The Shadow
of the CROSS

Morton F. Rose

BROADMAN PRESS
Nashville, Tennessee

Unless otherwise indicated, all Scripture references are from the King James Version of the Holy Bible.

All Scripture references marked (NASB) are from the *New American Standard Bible.* Copyright © The Lockman Foundation, 1960, 1962, 1963, 1968, 1971, 1973, 1975, 1977. Used by permission.

The reference marked (Phillips) is reprinted with permission of Macmillan Publishing Co., Inc. from J. B. Phillips *The New Testament in Modern English,* Revised Edition. © J. B. Phillips 1958, 1960, 1973.

The reference marked Moffatt is from *The Bible: A New Translation* by James A. R. Moffatt. Copyright © 1935 by Harper and Row, Publishers, Inc. Used by permission

Dewey Decimal Classification: 232.963
Subject Heading: JESUS CHRIST—CRUCIFIXION
Library of Congress Catalog Card Number: 86-9630
Printed in the United States of America

Library of Congress Cataloging-in-Publication Data

Rose, Morton.
  The shadow of the Cross.

  1. Jesus Christ—Crucifixion.   2. Crosses.
I. Title.
BT450.R67   1986   232.9'63   86-9630
ISBN 0-8054-5030-0

Dedication

To Ruby
the most faithful
and committed Christian
I know

Preface

Readers of certain books may suppose the origin of their content is found in sermons before they were prepared for print. In the case of this book the reverse is true. A manuscript was prepared for a book and then taught for more than ten years. The content has been rewritten many times; each time it was redone as a book manuscript and used as material for conferences and special Bible studies.

How many books have appeared which deal with the death of Christ? How many lessons on the cross have been taught? How many sermons have been preached on the crucifixion? Some may think enough has been written on the subject, but I doubt we can ever exhaust the meaning Jesus' dying. Possible help is found in one more book, written in a devotional and teaching style, which surveys those events leading to the moment Jesus died. From this venture may we have the experience expressed in Isaac Watts's verse:

See, from His head, His hands, His feet, sorrow and love flow mingled down; Did e'er such love and sorrow meet, or thorns compose so rich a crown?

Contents

Introduction: Dying Is Good News

Now I make known to you, brethren, the gospel which I preached to you, which also you received, in which also you stand, by which also you are saved, if you hold fast the word which I preached to you, unless you believed in vain. For I delivered to you as of first importance what I also received, that Christ died for our sins according to the Scriptures, and that He was buried, and that He was raised on the third day according to the Scriptures (1 Cor. 15:1-4, NASB).

The focal point of the gospel is that Jesus Christ died, was buried, and was raised to life. Paul declared that is the gospel he preached, which also is received, and on which faith stands firm. The death, burial, and resurrection of Jesus Christ comprise the gospel by which we are saved. That is good news!

J. W. MacGorman wrote: "Not until the death and burial gave way to the resurrection triumph over sin and death did we have a gospel."[1] We cannot separate the cross from the empty tomb, nor can we view all of the gospel without the cross. The death, burial, and resurrection are one event. That event, when received, and on which faith stands, is the gospel.

Every part of the Bible is significant. Yet all of it becomes a blur without the centrality of the cross, the tomb, and the bodily resurrection of Jesus Christ. The cross of Christ stands like a pinnacle to cast its shadow upon the world. The resurrection of Christ is that light of eternity which dispels all the world's darkness. All other events must be related to and evaluated by them. God has raised from death our Lord Jesus, Who is the Great Shepherd of the Sheep as a result of His sacrificial death, by which the eternal covenant is sealed. "Now the God of peace, who brought up from the dead the great Shepherd of the sheep through the blood of the eternal covenant, even Jesus our Lord" (Heb. 12:30, NASB).

Every spiritual experience can be measured by the death and resurrection of Christ. Every religious proposition stands or falls on the place given to these events in the life of Christ. Personal salvation is rooted here; doctrine starts here; living for Christ finds its motivation and power here; and the gates of heaven are unlocked by these master keys.

The name of Jesus is validated by His submission to His death on the cross. Let us unite our voices with that of the centurion when he exclaimed, "Truly this was the Son of God" (Matt. 27:54, NASB). The power of Jesus is magnified by victory over the grave. He lives forever!

> Living, He loved me; dying He saved me;
> Buried, He carried my sins far away;
> Rising, He justified freely forever:
> One day He's coming—O glorious day![2]

Never in human history has there been a death like it.

The emphasis in this book is on the dying of Jesus. In no way should we make the mistake of stopping only with the cross. Let us stop by the cross and experience its power. But be sure there is more when we go on to the tomb, to the resurrection morning, to the ascension, to Pentecost, to the missionary movement, to the first churches, to the promise of the second coming, and to all that God holds in the future.

In most parts of this book, familiar and simple truths about the crucifixion of Christ are rehearsed. Possibly a few fresh expressions will be found. The objective is to major on the death process itself, like a shadow falling over mankind. The reason for the title, *The Shadow of the Cross,* is to describe how Jesus died on the cross. *The Shadow of the Cross* shows the experiences of Christ in the step-by-step dying process.

Two key words dominate the book. They are *blood* and *death.* Both are unpleasant in human experience.

However, blood always attracts attention, and death is always news. Both words spell violence in today's society; but they always have. No apology need be given for identifying blood so strongly with Christ. Today's world sees too much a white-masked, compromised, and distorted Christianity. Blood is not to be viewed as bad or as a ghastly substance. In the Old Testament blood was seen as the source of life and regarded highly in Levitical laws. Blood was the life of the flesh and was given on the *altar to make atonement* for souls (see Lev. 17:11). In the New Testament we see Christ as the offering:

> "How much more will the blood of Christ, who the eternal Spirit offered Himself without blemish to God, cleanse your conscience from dead works to serve the living God?" (Heb. 9:14, NASB).

That same blood keeps life going. When understood, believed, and received, the blood of Jesus is the only hope for the world, and that includes that part of the world which calls itself Christian.

Death is a reality. Christ's death is not spectacular if one believes He only lived two thousand years ago. One could facetiously conclude that everyone who lived that long ago has died. Simply to commemorate a kind of death is not adequate. Death by crucifixion was horrid for anyone. Many persons died by that method in

Christ's time. No, we must do more than think of a great person who died young and by a cruel method. There is more than that to the death of Jesus. Joseph Klausner, an Old Testament scholar, has described a Roman crucifixion as the most terrible and cruel death which man has ever devised.[3] Added to that human terror is the much deeper suffering of a humanity separated from God. Such torture is not describable, and even the word *hell* is too commonplace in the language of today to grasp the meaning of the kind of suffering Jesus experienced. An adequate illustration cannot be found.

Therefore, *blood* and *death* are dominant in the content of this book.

The message in each chapter is intended to be devotional and inspirational. The secondary aim is to be instructive.

This book is in no way a theological treatment of the atonement. However, it should be clear from the start that any theological base for the thoughts in this book is firmly established on the authenticity of the Scriptures, the historicity of Christ and His Messianic consciousness, and a full respect and appreciation for the Gospel of John, alongside the Synoptic Gospels.

My approach is close to what W. T. Conner called "historic evangelical." Although Conner wrote that there were no theories of atonement as such in the New Testament, a reading of his book *The Cross in the New*

Testament (Broadman, 1954) provides an excellent reference for a theological study of the atonement.

Readers may be preachers, teachers, or others who want to read it for inspiration and instruction.

MORTON F. ROSE

1.

Death and Life

Try explaining the meaning of death to a three-year-old child. In fact, adults have difficulty defining the word itself. What is your definition of death?

> Passing away.
> Went away.
> Passed.
> Gone.
> Went to heaven
> Crossed over Jordan.
> His time came.
> God called.
> Slipped away.
> Deceased.

These words are not definitions; rather they are synonyms. We use three words in the place of the word death. Somehow it is painful to say, "My dad is dead!" Dying, die, dead, and death are hard and sad words. We do not like to use them. We do not want to face the reality of what these words mean.

The word death is defined as "a permanent cessation of all vital functions." The end of life! That is how Webster defines death.

Death, as seen by the human eye, and experienced by the human emotion is a helpless experience. What can anyone do about death when it has happened? That is the end of a person by all human measurements. Nothing can be done. What a helpless feeling!

Mrs. Holt had cancer. As I stood by her bedside in that moment of her death, there was nothing I could do. Her son wept and beat on the wall of the hospital room. What more could he have done?

Word came that Mr. Haber had died unexpectedly from a blood clot while recuperating in the hospital. I had the task of taking the sad news to his sick wife at home. When I told her as best I could, she wanted to pray. What more could have been done?

Mr. and Mrs. Carpenter had a son who died from a birth damage to the brain when he was seven months old. Two years later their second son died at the same age for the same reason. At the second death Mrs. Carpenter sat and stared during her grief. What more could have been done?

Reactions to death will vary, each person reacting in his own way. Yet, the most desirable reaction (whatever it may be) does not change the fact that death has occurred. To change that fact one stands helpless. D. P.

Brooks has written that human existence is bounded by birth and death, and nothing has enabled man to avoid that final boundary. He says, "Even the medical messiahs in white coats who have done so much to delay death have not been able to banish death."[1]

When death comes to our relatives and friends, all that earthlings hold dear in the world of sight, sound, scent, taste, and touch are completely gone—all but memories and memorials, and even they are eventually lost for most of us after a few generations.

> I want to explain death, Little Brother,
> but I have no explanation.
> I reach out to you, wanting you to know.
> I have no magic words, and my
> heart aches with the pain I
> know you are feeling.
> Words often fail to show what the
> heart knows and feels.
> My brother, I would explain
> if I could.
> But all I can say is that
> I'll be there,
> waiting for you, reaching out.
> I will listen. I will wrap
> you in my arms and rock you till
> the daylight of understanding
> breaks through
> the clouds of the mystery of death.

This is all I can do my brother—
    all anyone can do.
Death leaves no answers.
Take the memories and live on,
    my brother, my heart aches for you
    and with you.[2]

Death is a tragedy. It comes too soon in early life. However, for a few people death may be a blessing when the physical anguish of living is too burdensome. If humanity could find a better way to relieve its ultimate pain other than by death, it would prefer it. The only experience in this life worse than death appears to be the *act of dying*.

Here is the point. If Christ came into the world to cope with human life it seems most reasonable He would confront human death. How He did this was the same way He approached every other concern of humanity. He experienced it and did something about it. Because humanity is so helpless in dealing with death we can turn to Jesus to believe and benefit from what He has done about it. His death attracts and deserves our full attention.

        And when I think that God
        His Son not sparing,
        Sent Him to die,
        I scarce can take it in;
        that on the cross,

> my burden gladly bearing,
> He bled and died to take away my sin;
> Then sings my soul,
> my Savior God to Thee,
> How great Thou art,
> How great Thou art![3]

(In dealing with the way Christ identified with humanity, we must be clear that He did not commit or practice sin in order to be fully human. He was the sinless Son of God who faced His humanity perfectly, and in doing so was unlike all of us. In chapter 3 we will deal with how Christ faced sin.)

Death: The Fruit of Man's Greatest Enemy

The fact of death, the reality of death, and the inevitability of death do not make it desirable. Nor does it make it good or right. We can prepare for it; we can understand its certainties; we can search for emolients to take away its sting, but to like it or want it? Never!

Death comes to all of us for one simple reason. We are living in this world. That living has an end called physical death.

Death was tagged onto the end of life by one man's sin. That death was passed on to all of us. "Therefore, just as through one man sin entered into the world, and death through sin, and so death spread to all men, because all sinned" (Rom. 5:12, NASB). The nature of our living is to bring it to an end. That is exactly the fruit of sin: death! *For the wages of sin is death* (Rom. 6:23).

We should know that sin is our greatest foe. Without it we would not have death. We cannot make sin respectable, but we can make death acceptable. We can sum up their relationship and turn to Christ Who can do something about both of these.

We more often are attracted to the result than we are to the cause of our plights. Most of us do not associate the fruit of our lives with the seed we planted earlier. The alcoholic seldom ever associates his problem with the real cause. Most of us are past masters at rationalization—finding a good explanation as to why we act as we do.

Death is a fruit, a result, an effect, a consequence!

Inadequacies, imperfections, distortions, perversions, omissions, disobedience, and abuses are a few terms to describe sin. Society is out of shape and misdirected because of sin. Each of us pays his sin dues and reaps his sin harvest. Sometimes we reap directly what we have sown indirectly.

The young minister is killed in an automobile accident by a drunk driver. Our sinful society produces that kind of fruit. Anyone of us may be a reaper simply because we are in this world.

We may also be a reaper of our sins directly from divine intervention. God is not pleased with our sin, and His judgment upon human affairs is sure. R. W. Dale has written a splendid message on "A Theory of Atonement" in which he provides an impressive illustration of God's punishment of sin.[4] You have a child who is the light and joy of your home; her voice is sweeter to you than any music, and her face is fairer and brighter than a summer morning. Her thoughts are as pure as mountain air; her life as stainless as mountain snow. She is on the threshold of womanhood, and the very flower and perfection of her loveliness and beauty have come. And a wretch, whose crime human language has no terms vile enough to describe, and human laws no punishment terrible enough to avenge—deliberately, by hypocrisy, by lying, by a deep-laid scheme, worked out with elaborate cruelty—betrays her trust, ruins her virtue, and then flings her from him on to the streets of a strange city. He has no compunction for his crime. If opportunity comes to him, he will repeat it.

Dale asks the question, "Tell me now, what ought to be God's relation to such a man as that? Ought God be at peace with him? Most of us would agree that God's righteousness and justice, as well as One who is the relentless enemy of sin, would not overlook such crimes. We know it is infinitely better that every sinner should repent, and receive God's loving forgiveness. We know God does not want one person to receive Divine retribution. But if Divine grace is not sought, not asked for, and not received, then Divine justice will be exercised. We will be judged."[5] "As it is appointed unto men once to die, but after this the judgment" (Heb. 9:27).

Sooner or later, one way or another, we live long

enough to gather in the fruit of our worst enemy. That enemy is sin. That fruit is death.

And to think: even the sinless One, Christ our Lord, did not get out of this life alive.

Remember this: Christ could have left this world without first dying. He was sinless. But when He pitched His tent in the human camp, and took upon Himself humanity, He also became the victim of living here.

> God has come to us—assuming a status and a position that was inferior to the very angels who were His subordinates—becoming mortal, taking upon Himself our very nature, born of a human mother, died at the hands of cruel executioners, all in order that we might live forever as His sons and daughters.[6]

When Christ went through the tent and entered once and for all into the most holy place, He did not take the blood of goats and bulls to offer as sacrifice; rather He took His own blood and obtained eternal salvation for us (Heb. 9:12). Man's greatest enemy also produced its fruit in the life of God's Son. He died, yet He committed no sin Himself. But the same thing which kills us, also killed Him. Sin! *Ours!*

Life: The Fruit of God's Greatest Gift

Mankind's first thoughts of life can go back to Enoch in Genesis 5:22-24. Here was a man who walked right past death. We may believe that he took one of his long walks with God and never came back. Enoch set the pace of life for us—to walk in faith with God.

To the New Testament believer the walk of faith transports us right into the grace of God. This faith saves us out of death. Being saved *out* of death is different than being saved *from* death.

Jesus said: "I am telling you the truth: who ever hears My words and believes in Him who sent Me has eternal life. He will not be judged, but has already passed from death to life" (John 5:24, Author's Translation). Jesus is describing what the fruit of God's greatest gift is: life. The kind of life He gives is born out of death! We are dead in our trespasses and sins without saving faith in Jesus Christ (Eph. 2:1). Sin pays its wages—death—but God's free gift is eternal life in union with Christ Jesus our Lord.

Life is what God is all about. Love is His method.

We see God working with purpose at the beginning of human history. His work reached its peak almost two thousand years ago. From the beginning to that peak there is a trail of love. "God so loved . . . that He gave His only begotten Son" (John 3:16).

A special quality of God's nature caused Him to make the supreme sacrifice of His Son. That quality in

His nature was His love. There is only one kind of love like that. God's love! "But God demonstrates His own love toward us, in that while we were yet sinners, Christ died for us" (Rom. 5:8, NASB).

Another part of God's nature caused Him to set a supreme purpose for this love. That purpose was life for every person in the world. There is only one kind of life like that. Eternal life!

Because of His life, God is the supreme life-giver. Love is His motive. Giving life is His method.

Therefore, life-giving is God's method for His work in the world. In the Bible this is defined as the reconciling act of God.

> Much more then, having now been justified by His blood, we shall be saved from the wrath of God through Him. For if while we were yet sinners, Christ died for us. For if while we were enemies, we were reconciled to God through the death of His Son, much more, having been reconciled, we shall be saved by His life (Rom. 5:9-11, NASB).

That is what God started out to do. He created in order to give life. That is, to give His life by creating us in His own image. Uniquely enough, to understand what God is doing today we turn to the creation account in Genesis. As the crown of His creation, God made man and woman according to His pattern (Gen. 1:31). God created the kind of humanity which could have the sort of life which only God gives. God made a "tree of life" to nourish the life He had given to mankind (Gen. 2:9).

Mankind wanted something else, thinking there was more to life than what God had given. Man gambled with his right to choose and lost. Death resulted. Romans 5:12-20 will again help us understand this truth.

Humanity lost. That loss separated man from God by death. However, God was not made loser; nor was God satisfied about mankind being lost. God set out to redeem all persons, even though the majority will doom themselves by rejecting His loving offer. Therefore, God has performed the task of saving humanity from death. God begins with death, the human enemy, and works to impart life to each person. This work of God is the act of rescuing humanity from what it is, and offering it a chance to become what he intended it to be.

Often "eternal life" is thought of in terms of a duration which begins after physical death. I take the position that eternal life is to be viewed in terms of a quality of living which begins with salvation and which continues throughout eternity. The time scope of eternal life covers our earthly existence now and heavenly existence later.

John 5:24 gives us the dimension of the kind of life God gives. "Truly, truly, I say to you he who hears My word, and believes Him who sent Me, has eternal life, and does not come into judgment, but has passed out of death into life" (NASB).

The point is this: What Jesus did on the cross is an essential part of the process of God's gift of life. This appears to be a timeless, unchanging process. The divine activity is reversed from natural life processes. We generally think life first, then death: life and death. Looking at ourselves and then looking at God we must think: *Death first, then life: death and life!* Natural life begins with birth and ends with death. God's life-giving processes begin with Christ's death and bring the birth of life which never ends. Jesus described this activity taking place in us. It is a new birth for a person (John 3:1-3). At the time of the new birth the person passes from death to life (John 5:24). This is eternal life into which one enters at the point of the new birth. Therefore, each person entering the new life may have this testimony; "And the witness is this, that God has given us eternal life, and this life is in His Son" (1 John 1:11, NASB).

In the sixteenth century the essayist Michel Monlargne wrote: "It is not death, it is dying that alarms me."

It is dying that alarms me!

Not "If"—but how? When? and where? are the questions.

How did he die? How did it happen? When? Where? These are our questions about who died.

"He died quietly in his sleep."

"He was in his late nineties, and was never sick a day in his life."

"He ate a good meal the night before."

"He was so peaceful and happy during the past few days."

"The doctor believes his heart just stopped. He wasn't aware of it."

How do I want to die? On my feet! Active to the end. Suddenly. No wasting away. No lingering suffering. No pain. No hurt.

A friend of mine described the death of a person and then said, "*If* I die that is the way I want it to be." I asked him why he said "if I die." He corrected the statement by saying, "I meant *when* I die." Unconsciously most of us have a feeling we will probably not die, or at least we have difficulty realizing that we will die. Daniel Webster wrote: "One may live as a conqueror, a king, or a magistrate but he must die a man. The bed of death brings every human being to a pure individuality, to the intense thought of that deepest and most solemn of all relations—the relation between the creature and his Creator."

Of course, no one has ever lived to tell how bad dying is. For even the knock of death's door is not the same as walking through that door. If death is the end of life (humanly speaking), then the final step through death's door is followed by the slam of the door behind that step.

The bad part of dying is often the experience of those who stand by and watch it happen to others. In this case dying is seldom sudden for the viewer. He lives the

process in such emotional agony that seconds and minutes last beyond normal measurements of time. The
empathetic identity of the bystander with the dying
person often imprints a lasting impression. What may
take only minutes to happen may last days, and longer,
in the mind and emotions after the death of a friend or
loved one.

In a real sense this point addresses itself to those who
view the dying of others rather than to those who experience it. Some people may avoid much of the former,
but none of the latter. However, the way we view the
process of death of someone else helps us more fully to
understand, appreciate, and respond to the way Christ
died.

For I do believe that dying for Him was worse than
death. Before He went to the cross He told Peter, James,
and John, "My soul is very sorrowful, even to death."
(Matt. 26:37).

How, when, and where He died has an immense bearing on how the gospel itself is formed. It is His dying
that sounds the alarm for human response. We must
look at the Son of God and have some kind of empathetic identify with His dying. In doing so we are filled with
understanding and emotions that last long enough for
His dying to fulfill its purpose in us. We cannot pass
over this by smothering it with everything else we believe and know about Christ.

Christ's death as an event was the most final act in
human history. However, on the cross He experienced

more than death. To speak of His death without first speaking of His dying would be inadequate.

The backdrop for our thinking throughout the following chapters is the dying of our Lord. He did not die quietly in His sleep at an old age after a peaceful and happy life. He did not even eat a good meal the night before He died. That Last Supper was sadly disrupted by the exposure of a betrayer. It was concluded with a farewell memorial.

2.

Why Crucify Him?

And they cried out again, "Crucify Him." And Pilate said to them, "Why what evil has he done?" But they shouted all the more, "Crucify Him" (Mark 15:13-15).

Why? Why? Why?

Some people believe the screams of the crowd for Christ's crucifixion were produced by totally irrational emotion; that mob-force overruled quiet common sense; that shouting replaced thinking. In judging that crowd we must not lose sight of a larger fact. This event was no accident but rather part of an eternal plan. "Throughout the entire course of the arrest and trial, Jesus was the picture of a man on top of the situation."[1]

True, the crowd did not know about the plan, but what happened then was not out of God's control.

First, Jesus told his disciples, ". . . I lay my life down, that I might take it again. No man takes it from me I lay it down of myself. I have power to lay it down, and

I have power to take it again. This commandment have I received of my Father" (John 10:17-18).

Second, Jesus confirmed to Pilate, "To this end was I born, and for this cause came I into the world . . ." (John 19:34).

Third, Jesus plainly declared to Pilate, "You have no power at all against me, except it were given to you from above . . ." (John 19:11).

Pilate's primary question was "why?"

Why should He be found guilty? He had done no crime.

Why should He be crucified? He had broken no laws.

Why should He be put to death? He had done no evil.

Why? I find no fault in him!

Pilate presented a more penetrating question when he asked, "Why?" Our first reasoning power starts with the question "why?" Each of us should ask that from time to time. We must not blindly proceed with our theology of the cross without asking Why? Why was the cross essential?

Christ's enemies had their reasons for His crucifixion. They wanted to carry out their plan to rid themselves of Him who claimed to be the Son of God (and He truly was!) (John 19:7). No longer did they want to be irritated by His nonconformity and teaching which they claimed stirred up the people (Luke 23:5).

The pity was that His disciples did not know the real answer to the question "why?" Do we know why He was crucified? Do I know why He was crucified?

His disciples were confused, and as if in a nightmare they struggled with the ignominious defeat the idea of crucifixion conveyed. To them death meant the end. Most of them fled into the night.

We must answer the question why—and have *the* reason He died. There is one. To understand it is exceedingly important. Every other fact or truth you may believe about Jesus Christ hinges on answering that question.

A trip to Gethsemane with Christ can give us several of our best clues in answer to the question, "Why was He crucified?" There were three signal events: The prayer in the garden, the rebuke of Peter for using his sword, and the capture and binding of Jesus.

Peace: That Is Why!

Jesus led His disciples to the Garden of Gethsemane for a season of prayer. To them prayer was a familiar experience. Notice how He asked most of His disciples to sit while He went on to pray. Not all of them sat and waited, for He took Peter, James, and John with Him nearer the place of prayer. He made the uncomplicated request for them to watch with Him.

Watch with Him? What did that mean then? Does it

mean that mankind now—the best of it—all the Jameses, Peters, and Johns—are to share in the vigil of waiting for a decision from God? What a decision! Jesus, in agony, prayed that His cup of death might be spared Him. How could the contents of a cup be emptied? Could man drink it and survive? Is there now any way a person can carry the burden of his own sin? How heavy is that load?

Jesus wanted to make sure of the answer, and He also wanted the models of all believers to become certain of the answer. They were to watch with Him. So, this was more than a prayer meeting, more than fellowship between the Son of God and the Father, more than checking a few heavenly signals. Infinitely more!

Many feel this was Jesus' hour of trial. I think not. This was the hour of *humanity's trial.* Can a human being carry his own weight of sin? If humanity could do so, Jesus need not have come to earth. The "cup of death" would not have been necessary. He would not have had reason to die.

If one can save oneself;
If one can correct one's errors;
If one can live a good enough life;
If one can bear the burden of one's
own sin . . .

Jesus would not have had to face the cross. The world needs to know that. Therefore, He fell on his face and prayed, "My Father, if it be possible let this cup pass from me; nevertheless, not as I will but as thou wilt" (Matt. 26:39).

After His plaintive plea, how strange that Jesus seemed to consult those three disciples to find His answer. He found it. The answer—No! Humanity cannot bear the devastating load of its own sin. All it can do is plunge into perdition under the strain. Yes! Jesus must drink the cup.

These three disciples had every reason to be alert and cooperative with Jesus—but they were not. He had urgently and passionately implored them to watch. Can you imagine Jesus personally telling you that His soul was "exceeding sorrowful, even unto death"? What anguish He must have displayed! Sorrowful even unto death! Look at His face—His whole countenance. Did they, even the choice three of His own selection, not believe Him? "Who has believed our message and to whom has the arm of the Lord been revealed?" (Isa. 53:1, NASB). Look at Him, Peter! Can you see Him "despised and rejected; a man of sorrows, and acquainted with grief"? You cannot watch with Him for one hour? You appear willing—but oh, so weak!

As Jesus trudged back to the heart of Gethsemane, no doubt He was deeply feeling the first throes of being stricken, smitten, and afflicted, as prophesied in Isaiah 53.

He prayed the second time. Again He returned to

discover His inner circle of disciples asleep. They had no acceptable reason for their slumber. Tragic!

Look at Him, James! Will you hide as it were your face from Him and esteem Him not? Gaze at Him, John, of all disciples, the one who loves Him so much! See how He bears our griefs and carries our sorrows!

No, they, like all mankind, cannot see, feel, or know about the cup containing our sin and death. All we, like straying sheep, have turned to our own devices. We cannot bear our own iniquity but sleep in our weakness.

The third prayer presented a clear answer, like an exclamation. Jesus had not changed His prayer. He was assuredly given no encouragement by His disciples to change His thinking. The Father had no reason to change His plan. The cup would not be removed from Jesus' experience. After the third season of prayer, the Master returned to His disciples as before, but this time He had a completely different approach. There was an eternal reason for what He had done.

After the Son of God agonized over the oppressive burden of the world's sin, nothing had changed in that world. What an example of how praying may only affirm an answer already known! Christ knew He came into this world to deal with our sins, and to do so, He had to bear them on the cross.

For the religious rulemakers in our day, the act of Christ after the third prayer causes them confusion. To tell them to sleep on and rest was completely opposite to His instruction the two previous times. "Sleep on now, and take your rest; behold, the hour is at hand, and the Son of man is betrayed into the hands of sinners" (Matt. 26:45).

If Christ did not want His disciples to sleep, why did He change His mind? Of course, the answer is apparent. Sleeping was not His concern. Rather, He had wanted them to pray with Him. Christ is more often wanting us to *do* something, rather than *not do* something.

Jesus returned to the snoozing disciples with encouragement for them, rather than a rebuke. For them to sleep while He prayed displeased Him two previous times. In their insensitivity, they seemed to have no notion of what their Lord was doing. Often we are cast in their mold. If Christ had not returned the third time with a different approach, the three men could have later instituted a new rule for life, attributed the new rule as the will of God, and chastised themselves and others for not keeping the new rule. The new rule could have been that sleep and rest are against Christ's will. Religious rules are established in that matter. Christ did not come to establish a system for us to earn our salvation. He knew there could never be such a system. This experience for the disciples is evidence of that. Even if they had developed new rules out of this experience, they could never have kept them.

For Jesus to tell the disciples to sleep on and take their rest appears to be an illustration more than literal instructions. Note how after He told them to sleep on, He said, "Rise, let us be going; behold, he is at hand that doth betray me" (Matt. 26:46). What did He mean by telling them to sleep on and rest?

Sleep and rest give us physical renewal; they provide new vigor; they wash out the tiredness and weariness of the old day; they bring hope for a new day. In our souls we need rest or peace. Without Christ we become weary with our sins and guilt. They drag us down to a dead halt. Finding peace from that burden, without Christ, is impossible. There is no rest for the tired soul in a struggle to overcome, outrun, or wash away our sins.

The world turns over and over in its own sin, fitfully trying to find its peace. There is none without Christ. Paul writes, "and, having made peace through the blood of his cross—by him to reconcile all things unto himself . . ." (Col. 1:20). With him we cease our struggle and find our rest. Heavy eyes can truly sleep. The heavy load is really lifted. Peace comes to the believer.

That is why he was crucified!

Power: That is Why!

As Jesus led His disciples out of Gethsemane down a narrow pathway they were met by a vast crowd of people. Judas was directing the crowd. What a crowd!

There stood Jesus between His sleeping followers and His angry rejectors. He stood in the center of sinful and divided humanity. Some were for Him, some against him. None really understood what He was doing. Hands filled with swords and clubs in front of Him.

Sleepy eyes behind Him. I wonder if anyone could see His face in the darkness of that early morning hour. I am glad Luke 22:44-46 appears in our text—even if some claim it was omitted from earlier manuscripts. I wonder if some of the sweat which became like great drops of blood remained on His face after His agonizing prayer. A medical doctor says the phenomenon of bloody sweat is well-documented. Under great emotional stress, tiny capillaries in the sweat glands can break, mixing blood with sweat. If so, I wonder if it could be seen on Christ's face? That would not be a pretty sight.

> He was despised and shunned by men,
>> a man of pain, who knew what
>>> sickness was;
>> like one from whom men turn
>>> with shuddering,
>>> He was despised, we took no
>>> heed of Him.
> And yet ours was the pain He bore,
>> the sorrow he endured!
> We thought Him suffering from
>> a stroke
>> at God's own hand;
> yet He was wounded because we
>> had sinned,
>>> 'twas our misdeeds that
>>> crushed Him;
> 'twas for our welfare that He was

chastised,
the blows that fell to Him
have brought us healing
(Isa. 53:1-5, Moffatt).

Then Jesus was met by Judas. They stood between the two crowds. There they were face to face. Judas looked at him; felt His face with a kiss. How easy it is to touch Jesus. He makes Himself available to each of us for whatever reason. Peoples, and even governments, have embraced Him and used Him for their own purposes. Even churches! Note that the betrayer worked both sides of Jesus. He was a disciple who also was with those who carried clubs and swords.

At this place let us look at the position in which we find Jesus. He appears helpless, weak, and powerless. He was not understood by His closest disciples. He was betrayed by a friend and treated like a thief by his community.

The earlier scene in Gethsemane was difficult for the disciples to understand. This scene was not. Their leader was being threatened; he appeared helpless and seemed to have no power.

Humanity has always understood the importance of power. Power means security, wealth, and prestige. Esteem comes from power. Christ had lost His esteem, and that made Him appear to have lost His power and prestige.

Now what does it do to members of a group whose

leader has no power? Generally one or more members take over the group or the members abandon their leader.

I believe one member, Peter, decided to take matters into his own hands. Here is where Peter really denied Jesus. He showed every symptom of taking over. Even if his motive were to protect Christ he completely misappropriated such motives. Peter could have thought he had the power to do only what Christ, Himself, had the power to do. That was to intervene with a power to change human history. If Peter succeeded he could become the leader in the event. Peter could have wanted to stop the whole affair and restore power to the group. Furthermore, he would not run or withdraw. Man's struggle for power generally does end in a fight. Apparently he wanted to stand his ground, to meet sword with sword, power with power, and force with force. Therefore he drew his sword to fight.

Peter's display of power for whatever reason was rejected by Jesus. Jesus stopped him, but not in the usual way. He repaired the damage. Then He told him to put away his sword (Matt. 26:51-52). What a demonstration of the earthly ministry of Christ! He came to repair the hurts we bring on each other. Certainly Peter inflicted pain where he thought it was justified. Is there any better cause to hurt someone in the defense of what is right or for the sake of Christ? Can we not have a righteous indignation which wipes away the injustice of evil people? How best can we use the power given us than to defend the very Author of our faith?

Christ was doing both. He was caring for that which was righteous and using His power to help the unrighteous. A feat only possible by our Lord. He can repair the damage we do to each other, and do it without creating more destruction. He clearly demonstrates the difference in how He uses power in contrast to how we use it. Peter drew the sword to wound, and kill the enemy. Jesus drew on His powerful love to heal and give life to the enemy. He used His power for the purposes for which He came into the world. He intended to save, not kill! He was not interested in saving His power but rather His people!

Note Matthew 26:53: "Do you think I cannot appeal to my Father, and he will at once send me more than twelve legion of angels?"

Think of it! A legionnaire in the Roman army was regarded as the best and most trustworthy of all Roman soldiers. A legion consisted of from 4,500 to 6,000 such soldiers.

No doubt a heavenly legionnaire is superior to any earthly one. They are angels: fearless, powerful, indestructible. One angel could do the whole job. But Jesus showed His authentic power when He declared that twelve times 6,000 could be called to battle at once! That would be 72,000 fighting angels . . . more than enough to eliminate the world's population at once. What power! Christ did not come "into the world to condemn the world; but that the world through Him might be saved" (John 3:17).

How Christ used His power remained consistent with that purpose. He has given us an example of how power is to be used. Power is needed for every endeavor. Certainly power is a necessity for life itself. Worldly power often is destructive. We have heard that "absolute power corrupts." Jesus had absolute power, and He demonstrates what can be done with it to save and enrich life. He wanted His power exercised to defeat sin, not the sinner! He wanted to provide life, not kill it! In doing so, He knew the power of His own death was the source of that life for all who believe in Him. His death provided our victory.

> Would you be free from the burden of sin?
> There's power in the blood;
> Would you o'ver evil a victory win?
> There is power in the blood.
> There is pow'r in the blood of the Lamb.[2]

That kind of power the world needs. I need it; you need it. Jesus died to apply that power to our lives, "the power of God unto salvation."

That is why He was crucified!

Freedom: That Is Why!

John's Gospel records (18:3-9) a meaningful scene of

Jesus and his disciples leaving the Garden of Gethsemane. Let us rehearse the garden exit.

When Jesus met the crowd He identified himself. In fact, He took the initiative. When He saw them He called out, "Whom seek you?" They answered, "Jesus of Nazareth." Jesus replied, "I am He."

Verse 6 records a fascinating reaction of the crowd to Jesus' reply, "I am He." They fell backward to the ground. A band of men and officers with weapons retreating from the lowly Nazarene? Strange indeed! Yet, they were so hesitant Jesus had to prod them. He asked them the second time the name of the person they sought, and then after their reply He affirmed, "I have told you I am He."

This was not the first effort to capture Jesus. Before this time He always eluded those who would do Him harm. Before He always carefully protected His own freedom. Not so here. This was not a trap. He knew what He was doing. Jesus was in charge of His own capture, directing it by a prepared script, fulfilling every prescribed act. Never believe He was out of control! He had chosen to do the will of His Father. Pure freedom is the freedom to choose which of your alternatives to follow. Jesus was free to do the will of God. In Christ we, too, become free.

First, we are free to trust God to deal adequately with our sin and the death it placed upon us. This supplies us with a freedom *from* sin and its consequences. (Rom. 6:18) Jesus taught, "Not everyone who says to me,

Lord, Lord, shall enter the kingdom of heaven; but he who does the will of my Father who is in heaven" (Matt. 7:21).

A study of John 6:35-40 is helpful in understanding the will of the Father. Jesus gave three facts in this statement: (1) He came to do the Father's will, (2) the Father's will is that everyone who believes in the Son has everlasting life, and (3) the Father's will is that Jesus should not lose any of all those who believe in Him.

Jesus said:

> All that the Father gives Me shall come to Me, and the one who comes to Me I will certainly not cast out. For I have come down from heaven, not to do My own will, but the will of Him who sent Me. And this is the will of Him who sent Me, that of all that He has given Me I lose nothing, but raise it up on the last day. For this is the will of My Father, that everyone who beholds the Son and believes in Him, may have eternal life; and I Myself will raise him up the last day (John 6:37-40 NASB).

Second, it is a freedom *to* abundant life. This life is a present reality, as well as a dream of a future paradise. Jesus declared He was *the* way, *the* truth, *the* life. (See John 14:1-16.) Through Jesus we have the truth, and if we have *the* truth we are made free. "If the Son of God, therefore, makes us free we are free indeed." (John

8:32-36). This freedom is what we are free *to,* as well as what we are free *from.*

Third, it is a freedom by which believers can measure and judge their values in living. In Christ, by Christ, and through Christ I can choose my ethical and my moral behavior. He is the rule book for living, the Enlightener, the Motivator, the Empowerer. Political, religious, and social customs are measured and valued by this freedom. In Christ our resources are limitless, our potential is expansive, and our opportunities are boundless.

The event of meeting the soldiers in the narrow pathway leading out of the Garden of Gethsemane helps us see why Christ was taken and crucified. The key phrase in John 18:8 is in the words of Jesus, "If therefore you seek Me, let these go their way."

Jesus was becoming a captive so His followers could go free, no longer to be slaves to sin. He was the only one in all that crowd who was pure, innocent, sinless, and guiltless. Yet, He was placed in bondage. Those who were sinful, those who were guilty, those who deserved bondage could go free because Jesus was willing to be "bound."

No wonder he said, "Let these go their way: that the saying might be fulfilled, which He spoke of, of them which you gave Me have I lost none" (John 18:9).

He was enslaved that we may be free from eternal bondage. That is why He was crucified.

Peace, Power, and Freedom

For years I have believed the three experiences of peace, power, and freedom are among the major forces which people of the world have always sought to meet their needs. Humanity has devised every possible scheme to achieve peace, power, and freedom. The gaining of material wealth and earthly authority is thought to be the best means to achieve them. Evidence of this can be seen everywhere, in all areas of life. However, material resources or position will not secure lasting peace, power, and freedom. In fact, apart from God they cannot be fully and satisfactorily achieved.

Jesus satisfies the wholesome and spiritually healthy needs so characteristic in all of us. These needs relate to the whole person. Peace, power, and freedom are essential strivings within every human being.

The three events related to Jesus in Gethsemane and His arrest point us to the cross of Jesus where He made peace, power, and freedom available to us. Let us summarize.

First, Jesus stated, "Peace I leave with you, my peace I give unto you: not as the world gives, give I unto you. Let not your heart be troubled, neither let it be afraid" (John 14:27). This is the inner peace which comes to a person who finds his rest in Christ. A study of the fourth chapter of Hebrews is most helpful at this point. This peace comes through the forgiveness of sin and release from guilt. "How much more shall the blood of Christ, who through the eternal Spirit offered himself without spot to God, purge your conscience from dead works to serve the living God" (Heb. 9:14). The prayer experience Christ had with His Father and the three disciples in the Garden of Gethsemane shows us this truth, giving us one of our best clues to why Jesus was crucified.

Second, let us look at two of the Greek words in the New Testament which have been translated into the English word "power." One means ability; the other means privilege or authority.

To have the power of God at work in me means to have the ability to enjoy the best possible life. Jesus told His disciples, "You shall receive power . . ." (Acts 1:8). Paul said his preaching was in demonstration of power (1 Cor. 2:4).

To have the power of God at work in me means to have the privilege of exercising the authority of God in my life, and you in your life. This is linked to the priesthood of the believer. That is, I have within me the power (authority) of choosing, directing, and acting without checking with any authority other than God. Some Christians misinterpret their authority to mean they have power over other people. Not so. God is the source of power (authority) over each of us.

We often face what is termed *ecclessiastical authority* or the authority of the church, and its official leader(s). What is the authority of such people in relation to our lives? Hebrews 13 may be interpreted by some to demonstrate that such leaders have been delegated by God to have authority over the congregation, and that the leader is accountable to God for the behavior of the congregation. I believe such an interpretation of Hebrews 13 which supports those conclusions is not consistent with the life-giving process which grows out of the gospel. Rather Hebrews 13:7 indicates that, because our church leader is a proclaimer of the Word, he is to give us that Word, which outlives his influence. The Word of God is our authority, not the proclaimer of the Word. The preacher of the Word is to be accountable for what he proclaims, not for what the hearer believes about what he proclaims (Heb. 13:17). The timeless Truth, Jesus Himself, Who is proclaimed, is the One to Whom the believer must submit, and follow.

The authority of the proclaimer-leader is found in that Truth which he shares, not in the office he holds. I also think verse 7 is interesting in showing how the proclaimer is to live what he preaches so much that he becomes an example by what he does, rather than an authority by whom he is in a church office. To such persons we gladly submit ourselves to their influence, and receive the blessing of being in their presence.

The event of Peter's using his sword, and Jesus' reaction shows us what Christ was about to do to Satan's power, and established God's power among all who believe in Him. The power of God is given to us as the ability, privilege, and authority for living the abundant life found in Christ. That is why He was crucified.

Third, freedom is interlocked with inner peace which

Christ brings to the believer, and the power he is given as a child of God. Jesus meant every person to be free. He is the greatest liberator the world has ever known. This liberation is made possible to us because Christ was willing to be "bound" for us. Nailed to the cross! What a captive He became so we can be free from death forever! He told those who arrested Him that night to let His disciples go free. We who are His disciples have been free ever since.

With this background of why Jesus died, let us move our thinking to the death process itself.

3.

Dying: Poisoned Cup

The reference in the New Testament to a cup is often a symbol related to sin or death. There are exceptions, such as the cup of cold water referred to in Matthew 10:42.

The Pharisees were compared to a cup which was clean on the outside, but within filled with extortion and excess. This was paralleled to whited sepulchers full of dead men's bones and uncleanliness (Matt. 23:25-27).

"The cup of blessing," a term describing a third of the cups used in the Jewish Passover, was translated by Jesus as symbolizing the cup filled with His blood which was shed for the remission of sins (Matt. 26:27-28).

Paul delineates the meaning of drinking from the cup in the Lord's supper—the cup symbolized the death of Jesus. Paul wrote that the cup represented Christ's blood. "In the same way He took the cup also, after supper, saying, 'This cup is the new covenant in My blood; do this, as often as you drink it, in remembrance of Me. For as often as you eat this bread and drink the cup, you proclaim the Lord's death until He comes" (1 Cor. 11:25-26, NASB).

Considering the death of Jesus, we need to understand how He died—what He saw, felt, thought, and did while He was dying. The act of dying is pictured by the act of drinking from a cup. Jesus *held* this "cup" as He prayed in the garden of Gethsemane. When He went to the cross He *drank* from the cup. When He finished drinking, the cup was *empty*. These acts direct our thoughts to three fundamental truths about Christ's dying.

He Held the Poisoned Cup

The content of the cup is what created the need for the cross. If we are not careful we may think our Lord lived a life which was compartmentalized. The manner in which we organize our work today causes us to believe that a person must perform one specialized task within a specific work function. By this standard Jesus would have performed one task, stopped it, and gone on to another one until He came to the cross. This idea would isolate the cross from the rest of His life. It would make the cross only one of many phases of His life.

The entire life of Christ pointed to one central objective: He came to seek and save sinners (Luke 19:10) and establish His kingdom forever! Bearing the sins of the world was an essential part of His objective.

Jesus started filling the cup He held when He began His ministry. The time He started bearing the cup is clearly signalized early in His ministry (see Matt. 8:14-18). Jesus healed Peter's mother-in-law of a sickness. Matthew wrote that this was a suffering Messianic act by referring to the fulfillment of Isaiah's prophecy. Matthew stated, "Himself took our infirmities, and bare our sicknesses."

He did what?

He took and He bare! He carried with Him that which hurt the persons He helped.

Did He snap His fingers or wave a magic wand? Of course not! He could well have thought: *I will accept this person's pain and suffering. I will take and bare her sickness so she can be healed.*

He accumulated misery in that cup. His divine nature was moved with the most powerful kind of love that motivated His humanity to accept the burden of all mankind. No wonder John the Baptist proclaimed, "Behold the Lamb of God who takes away the sin of the world" (John 1:29).

Jesus was a human mop with a divine nature who swept across our sins and took them away. That is, He absorbed them. What a cup He carried to His death!

Let me draw a description of His walk to Golgotha. He envisioned this load of sin which was to be dumped on Him. How heavy the cross He carried!

Look at Him. Already bleeding, He leaves bloody footprints in the dirt. Smitten, He staggers as one with a broken back. Stricken, His head is bent in shame and disgrace. His eyes are blinded with the vision of dying like no human ever died. Lips parched. Tongue stuck to the roof of His mouth. He was carrying a curse unspeakable, a weight unbearable!

Every event in the earthly life of Christ finds its meaning right here. What was the need for Him to be born of a virgin, with the Holy Spirit as His progenitor, had He not the nature of God to carry the weight of humanity? What validity do those noble teachings about love and brotherhood have if He were unwilling to practice the supreme act of the love He taught—that willingness to relieve us of our pain by taking it upon Himself? How significant is the miracle of walking on water, if He did not, or could not, walk into the caverns of our hearts and there haul out the diseases which separate us from God? How important were His religious reforms like cleansing the temple, if He could not reach into the temple of every human being to cleanse them from their eternal corruption? Yes, the earthly ministry of Christ is to be measured by His act of carrying the cup of our death, and by what He did with that cup!

It is no wonder He prayed to rid himself of that cup. Holding it was terrible, but He did more than hold it! He was called on to drink its horrid contents.

Before the Drink of Death

The ninth hour came and it was noontime. When that moment arrived there was darkness over the whole land (Mark 15:33).

A dismal gloom shadowed the drink of death quaffed by Jesus. As the cup was tipped the scene was darkened. Jesus began the act which would change eternity for whomsoever should believe in Him.

Let us review together the last hours before He began the drink of death.

Many believe He was on the cross about three hours before noon. From the time Jesus was impaled on the cross until the noon hour, several remarkable occurrences transpired.

Upon reading the Gospel accounts, one can easily believe that at noon a drastic change occurred in the behavior of Jesus.

First, He literally was offered a liquid drink from a physical cup (Matt. 27:34). The mixture intended to ease the pain, a potion to render Him either groggy or unconscious. Some interpreters believe His followers offered Him this drink as a painkiller. Regardless who wanted Him unconscious, this act revealed they had no idea about the purpose of His dying. He could not, would not drink it. He tasted it, and it was the wrong cup. Of course, the cup from which He was to drink, which He "held" and carried to the cross, was not visible to the crowd. The cup He was holding was spiritual. Sin is difficult to ascertain before it does its damage.

Jesus rejected this physical cup which was offered when He was first put on the cross. He took this kind of action during His earthly ministry. He chose His suffering because of a purpose in coming to earth. Again, let us remind ourselves that Christ was not forced to the cross by the powers outside His control. Christianity was not born by rationalizing His death after it happened. No, the early followers, and later Christian theologians, did not need to create a reason why the Messiah was crucified, rather than becoming a King. The death of Christ is more than a symbol of a good man dying for a good cause. Christ was more than a martyr.

Second, He asked His Father to forgive those around Him (Luke 23:34). He saw two criminals hanging on crosses. There were a few disciples around the cross. Also there were those soldiers performing the act of crucifixion. Which ones needed forgiveness? For one reason or another everyone did. Everyone there at that time needed the touch of divine forgiveness. Also everyone, everywhere for all times. His prayer was to His Father for sinners. This was so much like every other act Jesus did during His earthly ministry.

One of the most profound, yet practical, books I have ever read is *Forgive and Forget* by Lewis Smedes. The subtitle is "Healing the Hurts We Don't Deserve." Smedes writes, "Forgiveness is God's invention for coming to terms with a world in which, despite their best intentions, people are unfair to each other and hurt each other deeply."[1]

As we review the crucifixion of Christ we easily recognize how unfair it was for Him. The pure, sinless, and perfect Son of God did not deserve the humiliation He experienced on earth, much less the treatment He received from the Garden of Gethsemane to the cross. How unfair! We can never understand how those who championed His death could not see how unfair and unjust they were toward Jesus. They were unconcerned about His being treated cruelly; but rather they might have thought justice was being done. Many had believed He was a blasphemer of God, and for that people were crucified. Those people were hurting the Christ of God, but believed they were helping themselves by executing remedial justice. Their doctrine of equity would stand up in the courts of religious law for that day. Perhaps they thought they were being fair! We know better now; Christ knew better then. His forgiveness of those inflicting the hurt He did not deserve was at the core of His dying.

Third, Jesus gave a specific response to the repentant thief. He did indeed save him. "Today, shalt thou be with me in paradise" (Luke 23:43).

In front of the believer is life, forever! The cross made the difference. Here were two sinners dying on crosses next to Jesus, at the same time being crucified by the same people. Yet, both thieves, like all of us, still needed Jesus to take them beyond that point. Our Lord, as He hung on the cross, responded to the one repentant thief exactly as He did during His earthly ministry. What chance could a person have with all his life behind him and none of it in front of him? In Christ, for all of us, the old spiritually dead existence dies, and is put behind us. "Therefore, if any man is in Christ, he is a new creature; the old things passed away; behold new things have come" (1 Cor. 5:17, NASB).

The mystery of the new birth experience if focused at this juncture in the life of a person. We must remember that the transactions of God are not proven by an objective scientific method. I cannot separate myself from such an event as spiritual conversion and objectively observe it in its process. "Each believer has the witness in himself; the one who does not believe God has made Him a liar, because he has not believed in the witness that God has borne concerning His Son. And the witness is this, that God has given us eternal life, and this life is in His son" (1 John 5:10-11, NASB).

Exactly how God makes a new spiritual nature within the believer cannot be understood by natural reasoning. Faith, and faith alone, provides us with our answers. Paul writes:

> And my message and my preaching were not in persuasive words of wisdom, but in demonstration of the Spirit and of power, that your faith should not rest on the wisdom of men, but on the power of God. Yet we do speak wisdom among those who are mature; a wisdom, however, not of this age, nor of the rulers of this age, who are passing away; but we speak God's wisdom in a mystery, the hidden wisdom, which God predestined before the ages to our glory; the wisdom which none of the rulers of this age has understood; for if they had understood it, they would not have crucified the Lord of glory; but just as it is written

things which eye has not seen and ear has not heard, and
which have not entered the heart of man, all that God has
prepared for those who love Him. For to us God revealed
them through the Spirit; for the Spirit searches all things,
even the depths of God . . . But the natural man does not
accept the things of the Spirit of God; for they are foolishness to him, and he cannot understand them, because they
are spiritually appraised (1 Cor. 2:4-11,14, NASB).

Fourth, Mary, the mother of Jesus, always seemed to
be at the right place, but without many words. What she
did spoke enough! Would Mary have preferred to be
dying in the place of her son? Likely so! She was a
mother. She was *His* mother. She knew Him before any
other human being. She knew Him intimately, like no
other human being. She loved Him as her son, her
firstborn!

She had stood alone before God and pondered the
mystery of the birth of this son. She was *found with
child of the Holy Spirit* (see Matt. 1:18). The Scripture
explains that her conception was of the Holy Spirit
(Matt. 1:20). Only God could make it possible for Mary
to bear His child. She had been a virgin. What a child
she bore! She would always claim Him as hers! Always!
As He hung on the cross, would she not have substitut-
ed her life for His? But, she could not do it. Jesus made
that clear to Pilate when He was on trial: "Pilate therefore said to Him, 'So you are a king?' Jesus answered,
'You say correctly that I am a king. For this I have been
born, and for this I have come into the world to be
witness to the truth. Everyone who is of the truth hears

my voice' " (John 18:37, NASB). Christ knew His kingship included His death on the cross, and no one else was able to be a substitute for Him, not even His mother.

Furthermore, Mary too was a sinner who needed the Savior. For some people this statement is offensive. Mary was not divine. She was 100 percent human. She was chosen of God, blessed of God, set aside by God, and served God. However, in her humanity, Mary was a person who needed the atonement like all the rest of us. Jesus looked at her from the cross and again acted in character with His earthly ministry. He cared for his mother. "Then said he to the disciple, 'Behold thy mother!' And, that disciple took care of her from then on" (John 19:27).

About that time we may assume it was noon. Now the whole scene changed. To that point while on the cross Jesus was seen and heard in the manner He had lived during His earthly ministry. At the noon hour that changed!

The Cup Is Emptied

So many churchgoers, Bible readers, religious persons express dismay to think that Christ ever drank from that cup of sin and death. Again, let me accent the fact that Jesus did not commit sin. He was presented the temptation by Satan, but overcame it (see Matt. 4:1-11).

However, as Jesus hung on the cross we can believe that the cup was tipped, and its contents was funneled into His life. First Peter 2:24: "Who his own self bare our sins in his own body on the tree . . ."

A stronger statement is 2 Corinthians 5:21: "For He hath made Him to be sin for us . . ."

As we view the spiritual experience of Christ on the cross we can view with the imagination a gigantic funnel over Him. The cup begins to empty. The content is sin. It boils with violence and destruction. How sin destroys! Here we behold all the sin of the world accumulated. As the cup empties it discharges its devastation.

Sin hurts! Oh, how it hurts. Look at the suffering. Every place sin touches there is a poison which exterminates; a catastrophe which annihilates; a sickness which putrifies! Nothing survives sin that is unabated and unchecked. It is deadly. It is fatal.

And Jesus accepted every vestige of the world's sin in His own body. And He received that on the cross.

How many times can one man die? Only once. Yet in the agony of dying Jesus suffered untold deaths, death for every man, woman, and child in the history of world.

Hebrews 9:26-28 gives us a picture of Jesus as the Bearer of humanity's sin. It was a one-time experience. The dose of all sin was compressed into that cup, in one event. We cannot begin to imagine the bitterness to Him who had never tasted one sin? This was infinitely more than a physical transaction. The very soul of Jesus was yanked into this affair. What a man! What a Savior! Once and for all.

The sin question was settled there. How many people who claim they trust Christ never fully realize that their sin has been put away? They still try to carry a load they cannot handle. The religion of rules, of ritual, of systems, of do-gooding cannot satisfy our need to have the load of sin removed! Only Jesus Christ can do that. Christ did not die for us in vain (Gal. 2:21). The burden of guilt is no longer ours to carry. He does for us what we cannot do for ourselves.

What other alternatives are available to rid us of sin? No one else, nothing else promises us that, "if we confess our sins, he is faithful and just to forgive us our sins, and to cleanse us from all unrighteousness" (1 John 1:9). That transaction is made possible by what Jesus did with our sin by His death.

Christ drew us to Himself on the cross. On the cross Jesus became strikingly human. He became sin for us (see 2 Cor. 5:21).

Several incidents transpired during the three hours Jesus was dying. Some of them are significant in understanding how Christ viewed the world from the cross.

First, he cried, "I thirst" (John 19:28). That morning He refused a drink. That afternoon He called for one. A human need of thirst surfaced above the pain of the pierced hands and feet; the aching trauma of thorns in His brow; the slashes in His sore back which had swollen the flesh. He was weak from the loss of blood. Add that to a heart which was being squeezed dry with sin. With this came the cry, "I thirst." The Scriptures indicate that all things had been accomplished when He asked for a drink. He pled for relief. He looked to the world for help. Like we often do when in despair, He acted like every other human. So different was He during this time than when He was performing His earlier ministry. While dying He sounded so much like all of humanity. "I thirst." "I need." "I want."

The world responded with vinegar. Regardless of the effect this mixture could have had in easing His pain, it was bitter. A thirsty person would not want sour wine, or any form of vinegar, to quench his thirst. If this were an effort to help him—and there is reason to doubt that it was—then the effort failed. The world will always fail. Remember, He was acting like I would act hanging there. He drank that stuff! "Now there was set a vessel full of vinegar: and they filled a sponge with vinegar, and put it upon hyssop, and put it to his mouth. When Jesus therefore had received the vinegar, He said, 'It is finished:' and He bowed His head and gave up the ghost (John 19:29-30).

Carefully note that our sin, which He had taken upon Himself, was responsible for His response on the cross. His identity with us was so close that "God caused Christ, Who Himself knew nothing of sin, actually to be sin for our sakes" (2 Cor. 5:21, Phillips). When that sin was taken by Christ He was fully aware of the event. He had willingly submitted Himself, and to believe He had been rendered unconscious before then is to make Him a victim, not a willing substitute. The same would have been true had He received our sin simultaneously with death. Sin is what killed Him. In the process of bearing our sin, He took on our character and responded to life's tragedy the same as we do. We cry out for help, for relief, for comfort.

Our search is often so desperate that we turn to the most immediate relief, or the most available fulfillment of our need. Frantically we grab the first thing which may have promise. Too often it is no more than a cup full of vinegar, and after we have taken it we wish we had not, because it was a futile effort. Like us, Christ cried for help, received what was given Him, but then died!

Second, at the ninth hour He yelled with a loud voice, "My God, My God, why have You forsaken Me?" (Matt. 27:46, NIV). Forsaken? Yes! God always separates Himself from sin! But, the other side of the issue needs attention. Understand that sinners choose sin, and by doing so make the choice to turn away from God. After doing so the sinner finds it easy to blame God for leaving him in a time of need. How many times have we heard the question, "Why has God done this to me?" Accusing God of forsaking us after we have made the separating choice is characteristic of a sinner. Jesus looked and acted just like us as He hung on the cross bearing our sins. No wonder He asked for the cup to pass from Him as He prayed in the Garden of Gethsemane! The Father turned His head away from looking at that composite of the world's sin. At that moment Jesus cried like all of us would throughout eternity if separated from God!

At this point we would do well to consider the eternal consequences of one's failure to exercise a faith which unites one with God. Such a failure cannot be justified by believing that God is too loving to let a person be separated from Him. This very act of Christ's dying on the cross will be the loving feature in God's nature which condemns every non-believer. God's love for His Son, because of this dreadful experience of taking our sins upon Himself, will be the dominant love-force which will separate a person from God. Yes, God loves His Son too much to let anyone disregard Him and what the Son did on the cross. When unbelievers appeal to God's love as their excuse for lack of saving faith, they are pronouncing a judgment upon themselves. God's love is too abundant for His Son to accept anyone who rejects Him.

Third, Jesus yielded. He accepted it. Unlike anything He had ever done. Ever! He gave out. The last human act is to quit living. You do nothing else in this life after that. You are through. Done. Finished. He yelled, "It is finished" (John 19:30). How much more unlike God could He have been? How much more human could He have been? He drank from the poisoned cup of death.

Every human faces the death row of life. All our efforts to stop death, or even to prolong the process, have failed. In the span of time to prolong the average life of a person ten, or even twenty years, is not an overwhelming success in immortality. To think of eternity and compare it with a lifetime of less than one hundred years shows us our human frailty. Death is our ultimate enemy. Humanity cannot survive its onslaught. We must reach that point at the end of all our endeavors. Death is life's final failure. Christ lived as a human only a little over three decades. His primary work as an adult lasted for only three years. But even the Son of God accepted the human limits, and for us He died.

4.

Dying: Shedding of Blood

When Jesus instituted the Lord's Supper He explained what drinking from the cup meant. "For this is my blood of the New Testament, which is shed for many for the remission of sin" (Matt. 26:2). When describing the act of dying and its relationship to blood, the Scriptures use the word *shed*. This word has a profound meaning as we look at Christ's dying process.

Nowhere in the Bible is the word "bleeding" used in relationship to the death of Christ. In the New Testament the word "shedding" or "shed" is used: "And almost all things are by the law purged with blood; and without shedding of blood is no remission" (Heb. 9:22).

Is there a difference between bleeding and shedding? Possibly so. Let us review a dictionary definition of the two words.

The word "bleed" as a verb means to emit or lose blood. The literal use of the word "bleed" can only be employed in relationship to blood. Even when used in other frameworks, its origin goes back to the idea of taking or giving blood.

The word "shed" means to set apart, to give off, to cast off, to eject, to spill, or to pour out. This verb has no particular relationship to blood. The word itself does not indicate what is being shed but simply describes the act of separating.

When we think of the Christ's dying, we see Him shedding His blood, which required bleeding. However, this was an act initiated by Christ. He was setting His blood apart—pouring His blood out. Too much cannot be made of the self-givingness of His death. His dying was God's doing, carrying out His plan. The blood shed on the cross is viewed as Christ's pouring out His life, rather than humanity's snatching that life away from Him. "No man has taken it away from Me, but I lay it down on My own initiative. I have authority to lay it down, and I have authority to take it up again. This commandment I received from My Father" (John 10:-18, NASB). He was doing that. His shedding of blood was a part of dying. He of course experienced the process of bleeding while He died—and after He died.

Without even emphasizing the different stages, it is vital to note how He bled before and after He died. The sequence of events is recorded in John 19:30-37. After Jesus "bowed His head and gave up the ghost" (v. 30), and before His body was taken from the cross "one of the soldiers with a spear pierced His side, and forthwith came there out blood and water" (v. 34).

Before He died He shed His blood, an act of His submission to the Father's will for Him to go to the cross. This pre-death bleeding was Christ's pouring out His blood. He shed it for the purposes discussed later in this chapter.

After He died (John 19:33) the soldiers thrust a spear into His dead body, and blood came forth. That act drew blood from Him. Here we see how humanity did its part in taking the life-blood from Him. The post-death bleeding was humanity taking His blood, rather than Christ shedding it.

The meaning of this will also be discussed in detail later in the chapter.

The Bible teaches clearly, without any compromise, God's everlasting antagonism toward sin, and the eternal consequences which He has decided will follow it. He does not, however, sit above the sinner with an all-watching eye waiting to catch him as a victim of His wrath. Rather, He comes out of His heavenly loftiness to the sinner's earthly sin-prison, and in doing so seeks to deliver him from the destruction which awaits him.

God's ultimate and greatest act of coming to rescue humanity was Christ's dying. Not only did He come to earth, and live humbly among men, going about doing good and healing all those who were oppressed by evil, He died in a manner which supremely fulfills God's love. He did all this for humanity while it was undeserving. "While we were yet sinners Christ died for us" (Rom. 5:8). His shedding of blood sealed the new relationship which can exist between a sinner and God. Jesus called this the new testimonial of that relationship. "After the same manner also he took the cup, when he had supped, saying, This cup is the new testament in my blood . . ." (1 Cor. 11:25).

Christ's act of shedding His blood is the means of our salvation. He is our new and living avenue to God (Heb. 10:20). This access is ours by placing faith in Him. "Whom God hath set forth to be a propitiation through faith in his blood, to declare his righteousness for the remission of sins that are past, through the forbearance of God" (Rom. 3:25).

We must join those who place their faith in Him. Otherwise we stand with him who pierced Christ's side after His death. In this crowd people stand outside the influence of His shed blood and join those who remain guilty in their sins. This is what made the cross necessary in the first place. To be in that crowd is to thrust a sword into the side of Him Who had died for us; and to reject Him is to slap His sacrificial love in the face. Do you want to poke fun at the Son of God as He hangs on the cross, dead in your trespasses and sins? If so, then, it must be stated that you reject His shed blood, and that you "know assuredly, that God has made the same Jesus, whom you have crucified, both Lord and Christ" (Acts 3:36).

We may question how much He bled. One drop of blood from one so great could have satisfied divine justice or representative atonement or vicarious substitution or anything else. However, to satisfy Christ's love it required more than a few drops of His blood. It demanded all His being and all His life. That was the totality of His life. It was sufficient to save a world.

Another question: Did Christ bleed enough for that alone to kill him? The purpose of His bleeding was to give us life. Sin opened the wound; sin squeezed the life blood out of His body. He died spiritually from the load of sin, and physically from the lack of blood. The physical shedding of His blood was united with a deep spiritual transaction. This shows the wholeness of the Son of God as divine and human. Both His Deity and humanity suffered from the onslaught of sin and death. What a price for Him, who knew no sin and deserved no hurt, had to pay! Neither His love nor grace come cheaply. This is the reason the New Testament makes so much of Christ's shedding His blood. The shedding of His blood provides for us a satisfaction of our deepest spiritual needs. Let us look at how His shed blood does this.

The blood of Christ is shown to obtain the spiritual satisfaction for which humanity hungers. We have looked at three of our greatest needs: peace, power, and freedom. The blood of Christ performs certain spiritual functions to meet these needs. We can find peace through the reconciliation made possible by the death of Christ. We are empowered by what the Bible shows as the "weakness" of Christ's submission to the cross.

Then, we are freed from the guilt of sin through remission by His blood.

Peace Through Reconciliation

Based on Colossians 1:20-22 the blood of his cross gives peace:

> And, having made peace through the blood of the cross, by him to reconcile all things unto himself; by him, I say, whether they be things in earth, or things in heaven. And you, that were sometimes alienated and enemies in your mind by wicked works, yet now hath he reconciled in the body of his flesh through death, to present you holy and unblameable and unreproveable in his sight.

The warfare waged by man against God is over. Peace is secured for the believer in a complete reconciliation, made possible by the defeat of sin in our lives through the blood of his cross.

Our wicked works had cut us off from God. This alienation made God our enemy. The cold, harsh statement that God has been made our enemy is not pleasing. Most people would claim they view God as a friend, not an enemy, and if He is our enemy, that is His doing, not ours. But we must take note it is our natures, our attitudes, and our actions which drive us away from God. We have done, and continue to do, the separating. After the separation we look upon Him as being against us. What a familiar attitude. Little children are taught that God will "get them" or will not love them, if they are not good. A child soon feels "not good." So that means "not-good" people should stay away from God. God is made a person's greatest enemy. At this point we must carefully underscore the responsibility we have for this alienation. God never designed that anything or anyone in His creation should have ever been alienated from Him. "The Lord is not slack concerning his promise, as some men count slackness; but is longsuffering to us-ward, not willing that any should perish, but that all should come to repentence" (2 Pet. 3:9). However, the Bible teaches us that God loves all "not-good people." He does not want to be made an enemy of anyone. Nevertheless we make Him exactly that in our minds when we see our wicked works.

"For all have sinned and come short of the glory of God" (Rom. 3:23). Every person needs to be at peace with God because of the failure to meet God as He comes to us. We, by nature, run from God. Adam hid from God when he had sinned. Humanity feels uncomfortable even at the reverent mention of God's name. Sin is a natural divider, and when pressed it drives us away from God. In our spirits we can easily become antagonistic to God when we are cut off from Him by our sin. This kind of condition destroys the avenues of building peaceful and lasting relationships. Forgiveness and reconciliation are needed. Christ has effected that through the blood of His cross.

73

We may ask, "Why the blood?" In Colossians 1:22 we have the answer: "In the body of his flesh through death, to present you holy and unblameable and unreproveable in his sight." This statement links Christ's death to His birth and shows the vital truth of His entire earthly life. His humanity touches His divinity from birth to death. Every moment from the cradle to the cross He was with us. "Behold a virgin shall be with child, and shall bring forth a Son, and they shall call His name Emmanuel, which being interpreted is, God with us" (Matt. 1:23).

He was the Word, which was and is God, made flesh and dwelling among us (John 1:1,14). Made flesh full of grace and truth. Where else in the New Testament is "flesh" spoken of in such a manner? Paul describes "flesh" as being in conflict with God (Romans 8:1-13). Was Christ who was made flesh and dwelt among us in conflict with God? No!

Some years ago I concluded from a study of Philippians that the law corresponds to the "nature of man." In Phil. 3:3-9 law and "flesh" appear to be closely related. Some believed that through keeping of the law one finds union with God. Paul wrote that such an effort is the work of the flesh.

> Though I might also have confidence in the flesh. If any other man thinks that he has whereof he might trust in the flesh, I more . . . touching the righteousness which is in the law, blameless. But what things

were gain to me, those I counted loss for Christ
. . . Yea doubtless, and I count all things but loss for
the excellency of the knowledge of Christ Jesus my
Lord . . . and be found in him, not having mine own
righteousness which is of the law, but that which is
through the faith of Christ (Phil. 3:4,6-9).

Paul also declared that such efforts of righteousness
are doomed to failure, and are at best considered "self-
righteous." Speaking of Israel he wrote: "I bear them
record that they have a zeal of God, but not according
to knowledge. For they being ignorant of God's righteousness, and going about to establish their own righteousness of God. For Christ is the end of the law of
righteousness to every one that believes" (Rom. 10:2-4).
We cannot keep the law. The "nature of man" (flesh)
strives to establish its own righteousness which ignores
God, because man cannot keep God's law. This makes
us aliens from God. We are cut off!

Christ is the only human who ever kept God's law.
He worked in absolute harmony with His Heavenly
Father. He completed what God started in the garden
of Eden. He is the one Paul calls the "last Adam" in 2
Corinthians 14:45. "For as by one man's disobedience
many were made sinners, so by the obedience of one
shall man be made righteous" (Rom. 5:19). His "flesh-
ly" efforts were perfectly successful. He broke not one
of God's commandments. He is the only who stands
before the Father "in the body of His flesh" with righ-

teous works. He did, in the flesh, what we cannot do in the flesh. The more we try to justify ourselves by the power of the flesh, the deeper in debt we plunge (Rom. 4:1-4).

Our peace is made through the blood of His cross, and in the body of his flesh through death we are presented holy, unblameable, and unreprovable. (Col. 1:20-22). What a reconciliation! Made possible by the body of his flesh, His own blood.

What can wash away my sin?
  Nothing but the blood of Jesus
What can make me whole again?
  Nothing but the blood of Jesus

For my pardon this I see,
  Nothing but the blood of Jesus
For my cleansing, this my plea,
  Nothing but the blood of Jesus

Nothing can for sin atone,
  Nothing but the blood of Jesus
Naught of good that I have done,
  Nothing but the blood of Jesus.

This is all my hope and peace.
  Nothing but the blood of Jesus
This is all my righteousness.
  Nothing but the blood of Jesus

Oh! precious is the flow

That makes me white as snow;
No other fount I know,
  Nothing but the blood of Jesus.[1]

Power Through Weakness

When the human body gives up its blood, it becomes weak and loses its power of life. Christ became a weak human being that day.

Christ was crucified through a strange kind of weakness, as the world judges strength and weakness. Following the same pattern of His entire life He made our negatives into positives. He took little and made much. He was passive when aggression seemed more appropriate by our evaluation. How could He turn a weakness into a strength? Indeed this is a mystery for the human mind. Yet, in 2 Corinthians 13:4 we read, "For though he was crucified through weakness, yet he lives by the power of God. For we also are weak in him, but we shall live with him by the power of God toward us."

By hanging on the cross did He disgrace heaven? Was God embarrassed to see the blood of His son? Was the Son's weakness a shame to the Father? No! No! No!

The sight of Jesus' blood is a humiliation to humanity! Earthly creatures want a king crowned with life's glory, not covered with death's blood! The sight of blood is repulsive and at best only calls us to sympathize with those who bleed. When mankind looks upon the dying of Jesus and the sight of His blood, there is nothing to admire. He appears to be a most unlikely Savior.

This makes it difficult for the world to believe Jesus is the Christ. This becomes a stumbling block to the kind of faith so many people want. Christ's dignity is lowered in the eyes of those who want to behold power and strength. Some of those around the cross thought that if He did not save Himself, how could He save us?

How weak was Jesus? He was never a person who cowed down or helplessly retreated to a corner amidst conflict. He was never spineless or spiritless. To view Jesus as a mousey man full of shyness is to distort completely who He was.

Jesus had a divinely tempered spirit with serene firmness. He was full of peaceful steadfastness, never resigning to meaningless submission. He was always in control, always sure, always positive, always definite. Strong without flexing His power!

Yet, that was not apparent to those who viewed His dying. There He hung between two thieves, seemingly in defeat. All kingdom hopes for His followers appeared to be dying with Him. He looked whipped, and the gashes in His defeat bled profusely. That was the ghastly picture.

Would not modern-day newsmen have a field day? Imagine what color television cameras and news analysts could do with that scene. To them it surely would have been bad news but news worth covering.

We can imagine they would have tried to emphasize the man on the middle cross. They could have made His blood, His dying, His suffering no different from that of the other two nailed to those crosses. They could have challenged the eyewitnesses who believed, "This was the Son of God." They could have thought, *There is a man merely dying—powerless to avert his own doom, much less save others.*

Reporting the event does not always mean presenting the facts. There was power in that blood shed for the remission of sins—heaven's power, not earth's power. God's power, not man's power. Eternal power, not temporal power. Here was and is the Good News of God, not the bad news of man. The meaning of the gospel is found right here. Our response is evoked at this point. We hear the good news of this act fraught with possibility, and upon that we embrace Him Who has done so much for us. We can declare throughout eternity: "For I am not ashamed of the gospel of Christ: for it is the power of God unto salvation to every one who believes" (Rom. 1:16, NASB). The very power of this gospel appears to be a weakness to most observers. But to those of us who believe, it becomes our power. Power unto eternity, power graciously providing us life forever, power to do what can never be done any other way to change the heart of mankind!

We are to tarry here long enough to be ennobled by standing in the shadow of the cross. Here we are to find our life, and if one should chose to reject His gospel, one makes the cross a block of wood over which one stumbles into hell. Rejection means to perish, and in the unbeliever's destruction we look at the blood-drenched ground below the cross as a foolish waste. "But we preach Christ crucified, unto the Jews a stumbling block, and unto the Greeks foolishness" (1 Cor. 1:23). The world cannot back away from what it perceives as an unsightly scene in history. As we walk by this event, we enter into its meaning with a yes or a no response. There can be no casual observers.

Through the weakness of His blood emerges the most powerful transaction in human history—the forgiveness of sins forever, to all who call upon Him.

Freedom Through Remission

". . . and without shedding of blood there is no remission" (Heb. 9:22). Remission means dismissal or release, to be made free by the act of a pardon.

Is there any question that remission is needed, that every person is a slave to sin and is in bondage to spiritual death? How the human soul longs to be freed from such captivity!

Man cannot tolerate being subordinated or put under the power of an evil superior. Sin burdens us with fearful constraints and cages us. Like animals, lost mankind is in sin prison! When the will of man is chained by sin his spirit is broken. What will a man give in exchange for his soul? Sin forces everyone of us to make an easy swap. Give us temporal security, and we will relinquish some of our freedom. Give us earthly power, and we will forfeit our heavenly promises. Give us a moment of fame and we will discard our good name. How attractive the deal looks when sin measures the payment! What fools we are! "The wages of sin is death." With it goes subordination to principalities and powers which work against us. "For we wrestle not against flesh and blood, but against spiritual wickedness in high places" (Eph. 6:12) With it goes constraints and confinements not intended for those created in God's image.

We want out. But how do we get out? We can catch a glimpse of freedom only as the light of truth shines on the cross, and there reveals the blood of Jesus.

Remission of sin through His blood is a high price for freedom, but the price secures life for anyone who believes. Remission releases us from death.

Closely related to finding our freedom from sin by remission is understanding and experiencing forgiveness. Without a release from our past we harbor our guilt, and it festers in our consciences. This spiritual sickness compounds as we continue depositing new corruption in this sin bank. How ladened we become, and the burden is both heavy and costly! Only God's cleansing forgiveness can reach into those crevices of our souls and deliver us from sin's captivity.

The world should be sick on the steady diet of false promises to cure its sin-sick soul. Only Christ, who was crucified and raised from the dead, can provide the lasting satisfaction for that hunger which finds no gratification elsewhere.

Too often we major on what we are freed from after we secure our release. Looking back is needed only to keep us in perspective. We cannot live in that past. Believers have been freed. That is the point. What we have been freed to is now more important for our consideration in the future, than dwelling on what we have been freed from. We are released to live and to start that living on this side of heaven. Those who are freed know there is an abundance of living between the cross and heaven. We are released from sin with a design made by God. This design helps us with our sinfulness from then on. God begins working in us the likeness of His only Son.

> I will sing the wondrous story
> Of the Christ who died for me,
> How He left His home in glory
> For the cross of calvary.
>
> I was bruised, but Jesus healed me,
> Faint was I from many a fall;
> Sight was gone, and fears possessed me,
> But He freed me from them all.
>
> Days of darkness still come o'er me,
> Sorrow's paths I often tread,
> But the Saviour still is with me;
> By His hand I'm safely led.
>
> Yes, I'll sing the wondrous story
> Of the Christ who died for me,
> Sing it with the saints in glory,
> Gathered by the crystal sea.[2]

5.

The Meaning of His Death

Tremendous emphasis is placed on the birth of Jesus, and rightly so. Yet there should be more of His dying. That is why He was born.

Who can mark the time of His death and stop it? Who could climb up there on the cross and nurse the wounds and stop the bleeding?

How about Judas? Of course, Judas may have prevented it by not having betrayed Jesus. Oh, Judas! Stop the bleeding!

Pilate sentenced Jesus. Possibly he could have reversed his decision and rushed paramedics up the hill to rescue Jesus from the cross. However, their equipment could never have read the vital signs of eternity. The bleeding could not have been stopped by a medical expert.

The crowd around Jesus hollered, "Crucify Him." Why such intense emotional outcries? To blame the Jews with the murder of Jesus is in itself a type of religious bias. Judaism as a race or religion acted in the manner all Christless cultures of mankind do. It sought to preserve itself regardless of cost, including the life of the Messiah whom they would not claim. "He came unto his own, and his own received him not, but as many as received him, to them gave he power to become the sons of God, even to them that believe on his name" (John 1:11-12). Jesus went to His own and they would not accept Him (John 1:11). Since the earthly life of Christ, history records that even in His name, war has been waged and a so-called Christianity has been spread or preserved by the sword, burnings at the stakes, drownings, and other acts of murder. Political movements have often assumed the name of Christ, and in that name acted brazenly in a political and/or military way. Little resemblance can be seen in the pages of history between such political/military activities and the New Testament teachings of Jesus. In fact, such human activities have betrayed the exact purpose for which Christ died. That purpose is to usher in life (see John 10:10). The sad truth is: So many people have not known the difference between the purpose of Christ and the horrendous perfidy done in His name.

No, we cannot expect religion or religious people to stop the bleeding of Christ. For many it served their perverted purposes for Him to be executed.

The suffering of Christ was not the conclusion of God's plan for His Son. Therefore His suffering could not be exploited by anyone for any reason—nor could it be stopped.

Stop the bleeding? How could anyone have stopped that death process? Just as no one could have taken His life (without His willingness to give it), no one could have stopped the manner in which He died. Know that for sure. He dismissed His own spirit of life. John 10:18 describes the event of death as a controlled experience. Suicide? No! Self-sacrifice? Yes! He died by His own volition. No man could squeeze the life out of His body. "No man taketh it from me, but I lay it down of myself. I have power to lay it down myself. I have power to lay it down, and I have power to take it again. This commandment have I received of my Father" (John 10:18, KJV).

Crucifixion on the day before the sabbath was the worst kind. Generally, death was not experienced by the end of one day. The criminal generally had to be taken down from the cross earlier than at other times so he would not be on the cross during the sabbath. When this was the case, the legs were broken to insure that the criminal would not escape if he should revive after being taken down from the cross.

When they came to Jesus He was already dead. Breaking His legs was not necessary. However, a soldier ran a spear into His dead body. That violent thrust brought forth blood and water. The blood mocked the power of man. You cannot kill a dead person. You may draw his blood but you cannot kill him. No man took His life. He had already given it!

Jesus not only gave up the life which was sacred to

God, He also yielded that which was sacred to man, His blood. Now we move our attention to how many may view the cross. What does the dying of Jesus mean to us? What does His death demonstrate to us?

His Death Shows the Seriousness of Sin

Bleeding requires immediate and priority attention. A bleeding person must not be kept waiting. No one makes light of the pulsating gushing of blood from the human body. As Christ bled we realize He was telling the world to take seriously the meaning of his dying. His death displays God's estimate of man's sin. This historic scene requires a response today. We must be grimly serious about His death. Immediate and priority attention is required. No one could have stopped the bleeding, nor can we now erase the death of Christ. The call of the cross is not to make His death right, but rather to let His death make us right!

His bleeding shows the seriousness of sin.

For Christ is not entered into the holy places made with hands, which are the figures of the true; but into heaven itself, now to appear in the presence of God for us: nor yet that he should offer himself often, as the high priest entereth into the holy place every year with the blood of others; for then must he often have suffered since the foundation of the world: but now once in the end of the world hath he

appeared to put away sin by the sacrifice of himself
(Heb. 9:24-26).

The believer's conscience is purged by the blood of
Christ, who through the eternal Spirit offered himself
without spot. "How much more shall the blood of
Christ, who through the eternal spirit offered Himself
without spot to God, purge your conscience from dead
works to serve the living God?" (Heb. 9:14).

The cross eloquently tells the world that God took
the most extreme measure to deal with sin: the life of
His Son. Open-eyed persons readily see the attitude of
God toward sin. How serious do we take sin? See the
blood! Believe what it means. Have faith in Him who
shed it for an extremely important reason. The world's
sin made that bleeding necessary. Can we compromise
what caused God's Son to suffer so? Can we dismiss sin
as trivial after it inflicted such wounds? No! Sin is a
heinous business. Sin stays busy and performs its work
evilly and hatefully.

Sin is always active in the world. By many names it
keeps coming on strong. Its results reveal what it really
is . . . more than its inviting appearance.

But sin is not like fruit growing on a tree. It is like
a cancer growing on the brain. We choose to gather the
fruit and eat it. Cancer's growth gives us no option. Its
deathly presence gradually and surely does its work.
Sin's poison is in the life system of each of us! There is
no procedure to cut it out or wash it off or take self-

corrective actions. There is no method of excising sin apart from faith in Christ. His bleeding shows us that simple but absolute truth. So, look at the blood of Christ which cleanses us from all unrighteousness (see Eph. 1:7; 1 John 1:9).

His Death Shows Us the Will of God

Christ prayed about this experience. He asked His Father to take "this cup" away. After He made the request He then submissively prayed, "Nevertheless not my will but thine . . ." The will of God is that no one perish. Either Christ died or we perish. God's will is that we live eternally, and that was made possible only by the death and resurrection of His only Son. "And this is the will of him that sent me that every one which seeth the Son, and believeth on him, may have everlasting life; and I will raise him at the last day" (John 6:40). When we look at the bleeding of Christ, we suddenly see a concept different from mere bleeding, as terrible as that is. Romans 5:8-9 links God's love to His death and His shed blood. A bit of bleeding was not enough. He had to bleed to death. "But God commendeth his love toward us, in that, while we were yet sinners, Christ died for us. Much more then, being now justified by his blood, we shall be saved from wrath through him" (Rom. 5:8-9).

The absolute will of God in daily affairs is often difficult to determine. Yet, His will is prescribed in so many places as we turn to the Scriptures. Understand-

ing the will of God in relationship to the death of His
Son is no mystery. It is not necessary to ponder what
that will was. The Heavenly Father and His Son, Jesus,
both loved the world enough to transfuse that love
through the death of Christ into the world. What a
transfusion it is! That shows us the will of God in that,
"The Lord is not slack concerning his promise, as some
men count slackness; but is long suffering to us-ward,
not willing that any should perish, but that all should
come to repentence" (2 Pet. 3:9).

His Death Shows the Depth of Love

Being a blood donor is not easy. Most people give
away their blood; a few sell it. We are not to judge why
they give up their own blood. When one gives his blood
he feels that someone else will be helped and that he will
not be hurt. That is an excellent arrangement. However,
suppose a person had a choice. Give all your blood now
or your child dies! One pint will not do. "All or nothing
at all." Christ loved humanity enough to give it all to
save our lives. His gift killed Him. The blood flowed
through His heart of love and spilled over the sins of all
humanity.

William Adams Brown relates the following story:

> Many years ago a remarkable surgical operation was per-
> formed in New York City. It was a case of blood transfu-
> sion, the first of the kind, so far as I know, to be
> successfully performed in the annals of the profession. The
> subject was a baby, a little girl only a few days old, whose

life was ebbing away drop by drop from an internal hem-
orrhage that all the resources at the command of the
physicians in charge were unable to control. As a last
desperate chance, it was resolved to attempt a transfusion
of blood from the father to the child. The father's arm was
laid bare for more than six inches, and an artery extracted.
With infinite pains and patience this was connected with
a vein in the baby's leg and the current allowed to pass
from one to the other. Those who witnessed the operation
describe the scene that followed as one of the most dra-
matic in the history of surgery. The child lay by the father's side, a motionless object, waxen white; to all
outward appearance, dead. Presently a faint tinge of pink
appeared on the rim of the ear, then a glow suffused the
whole body, the skin grew normal, the fingers and toes
took on a rosy hue. Suddenly the lips opened in a lusty cry;
the cry which has been sounding in the ears of fathers and
mothers ever since parenthood began.[1]

That was literally a case of purchase with blood. But
it was not the father's suffering that saved the child; it
was his life that did.

Compared to the Savior's love, all other loves are
secondary and subsidiary. So seldom is His love understood, and then when it is, it is often rejected. The
growing experience many people call love has a simple
and disgusting definition. Briefly put, love is defined as
that which one does to, or for, another person to get
what one wants from that person. Under this definition
comes the entire philosophy that love pays the lover,
and in Christ's case love *cost* Him His life. "Greater love
hath no man than this, that a man lay down his life for
his friends" (John 15:13).

His death was timely in human history. "But when the fulness of time was come, God sent forth his son, made of a woman, made under law, to redeem them that were under the law, that we might receive the adoption of sons" (Gal. 4:4-5).

Everything was ready in human history. The world needed Christ. History was coming to its focal point for all time. Not until this period were all factors so favorable. The Jewish religion, Roman politics, and Greek culture formed the best historic cradle to receive the birth of Christianity.

The earlier spread of Greek culture broke both the language barrier and transportation limits. It expanded world trade. The walls of nationalism had been broken down. The track for spreading the gospel had been set. The Roman governmental system provided a type of world unity. Not until our own generation could a message be carried so fast in the known world. Thousands of people then traveled from Jerusalem to Rome frequently. Roman rule made such travels comparatively safe in the civilized world.

The Jewish religion laid the groundwork for the Messiah and His mission. Decades later Paul sought out the Jewish synagogues for his first preaching points. There he won many to Christ, most of whom were non-Jewish attendants of the Hebrew worship services.

This was the most propitious time in human history for God to perform His reconciliation act through His Son. From this time on, "There is to be neither Jew nor

Greek, there is neither male nor female: for ye are all one in Christ Jesus" (Gal. 3:28). The blood of Jesus makes all of us of one blood when we are members of His body. His blood eliminates all prejudice against minority groups. Racial, religious, political, age, and sex barriers are crossed, and the family of God is formed into one cohesive group. Because of this it can be said, "For you are all the children of God through faith in Christ Jesus" (Gal. 3:26).

The time was right.

The Right Place to Die

They came to a hill called Golgotha, thought to have appeared in the shape of a skull (Mark 15:22). It was a common site for executing criminals by crucifixion.

Execution by crucifixion was a slow process which was painfully exhausting for the victim. Death seldom resulted from the loss of blood. Hands and feet were either tied or nailed to cross beams of heavy timber. Jesus was nailed to the cross. He referred to the "nail prints" in His hands and feet after His resurrection (John 20:24-27).

Christ was worn-out and bleeding as He hung there. This method of execution was hideously cruel and beastly. The outstretched arms, the naked body, and the nailed flesh were lifted up on cross beams in full view of the curious bystanders. What a place to die! What a gruesome place for Christ to die. Was such a spot necessary?

Golgotha was both a place to punish offenders of society and to rid the community of law breakers and evil doers. "The hill of the skull" was Jerusalem's dumping ground for the wrongs it found in its midst.

Civilized communities have always struggled to eliminate their crime, their wrongs, their injustices. Crucifixion was like the gallows, the firing squad, and the electric chair. Crucifixion was a means of cleansing society of certain kinds of criminals. The death of a criminal would end his crimes. The presence of two criminals being executed alongside Jesus accented the meaning of Golgotha. The place where Jesus died was between two human beings judged as unworthy and undesirable. By judgment they were receiving the due rewards of their nefarious deeds (Luke 23:41).

Was that the right place for the Son of God to die? Those who do not understand the meaning of His dying would not think so, but Golgotha was the right place!

Seldom is crime thought of as the result of sin. But it is. Not all results from sin are considered crimes by the laws of man. Not all sinners are classified as criminals, but the reverse is always true. All criminals are considered sinners. There was no mistake that Jesus experienced a criminal's death. Everything about the place showed it.

Man's law is designed to wipe out crime. Even throughout history that effort was made by executing the extreme criminals. So, Christ became God's means of wiping out sin. He commanded His Son to lay down

His life (John 10:18). The cross was the appropriate place.

Nothing could stop His dying. The time and the place were right.

His Death Satisfied God's Divine Justice

The most obvious question is, "Why did not God stop the death of His Son?" One may wonder why the Father's will was not different, and when Christ prayed that this cup of death be removed, why not? Why did Jesus say, "This commandment have I received of my Father"? (John 10:18).

I am indebted to R. W. Dale's writings in Broadman's *Christian Classics, Nineteenth Century Evangelical Theology*[2] for insights as to how God's divine justice works. He develops his position as a portion of a treatment of the atonement.

We conclude therefore that the only concept of punishment which satisfies our strongest and most definite moral convictions, and which corresponds to the place it occupies both in the organization of society and in the moral order of the universe, is that which represents it as pain and loss inflicted or the violation of a law.

If the law is a righteous law, if the severity of the penalty is in proportion to the magnitude of the offense, the punishment is just; the offender has deserved whatever he suffers. Suffering inflicted upon a man to make him better in the future is not punishment, but discipline. To be punished, it must be inflicted for evil deeds

done in the past. Suffering endured for the sake of be-
nefiting society is not punishment. If accepted volun-
tarily, it is heroism of self-sacrifice; if inflicted by
arbitrary authority, it is injustice on the one side and
martyrdom on the other. What a man suffers from re-
sentment of another is not punishment but mere perse-
cution and annoyance, unless the suffering is the effect
of moral indignation provoked by real or imaginary
wrongs committed against the person by whom the suffering is inflicted. According as the wrongs are imaginary or real, the punishment is unjust or just.

Dale maintains that the suffering inflicted is a necessary element in the concept of punishment. Once it is
determined that God's relation to the sins of humanity
which has transgressed the eternal Law of Righteousness, then God must determine the suffering which may
justly come upon the transgressors. God cannot be separated from the Divine Law which has been violated.
This then affirms the principle that sin deserves to be
punished. Dale maintains:

> Such a separation, however, between the ideal Law
> and the Divine Will is impossible. God would cease
> to be God if His were not a complete expression of
> all the contents of the eternal Law of Righteousness.
> Is it then inevitable that God should inflict the pen-
> alties which sin has deserved? He had no choice.
> . . . The heart of the whole problem lies here. The

eternal Law of Righteousness declares that sin deserves to be punished.[3]

The execution of justice was fulfilled by God's laying
aside His eternal glory, assuming human nature in the
form of Jesus Christ, Who then being forsaken by God,
died on the cross, that the sins of humanity might be
remitted. Dale writes, "It belongs to Him to assert, by
His own act, that suffering is the just result of sin. He
asserts it, not by inflicting suffering on the sinner, but
by enduring suffering Himself."[4]

The death of Christ satisfied Divine Justice.

His Death Provides Assurance of Forgiveness

The most penetrating and meaningful intercessory
prayer made for all people was the brief statement of
Jesus, "Father, forgive them; for they know not what
they do" (Luke 23:34). Christ was familiar with abuse.
He had been rejected, falsely accused, and condemned
on several occasions. He had accepted and forgiven
those who wronged Him. Yet, not until His greatest
abuse did He so clearly state His desire to forgive and
to evoke the forgiveness of His Father. For most of us
this would have been a most unlikely time to be thinking
about others and to be wanting them relieved of their
guilt.

To forgive those who hurt others is one situation, but
to forgive those who hurt *us* is a completely different
matter. When a friend hurts someone it is easy to for-

give him. But, when he hurts *me* I am crushed. Jesus taught us to forgive each other. He expects us to do so. On the cross He validated His teachings by showing us that He practiced what He preached.

Forgiving people who are concerned about you, and care for you, and who did not want to hurt you, is one side of the coin. To seek forgiveness for those who hurt you, and do not care, is the other side. The person who hurt us and does not care cuts the first wounds of offense even deeper. Jesus looked upon a crowd and saw a majority who cared nothing for Him. In fact, they mocked in deliberate derision or uncaringly gambled for His garment as if He were not there. Christ included them in His request for forgiveness.

Some people are often confident that one only can survive being hurt by others through retaliation, and that accompanied with hate and violence. If it were not for what Christ did for us on the cross, maybe Divine Justice would be served by taking punishment into our own hands. Perhaps the religions which do not have the forgiving cry from the lips of Jesus find punitive justice their only way to deal with evil. They kill the evildoer and feel they have vindicated the victim of his evil. To seek forgiveness for the evildoer only makes sense when one understands what Christ was doing on the cross in the first place.

Now we can hear the promise: "If we confess our sins he is faithful and just to forgive us our sins, and to cleanse us from all unrighteousness" (1 John 1:9).

6.

Were You There?

As we review the death of Christ we dare not stop with only a backward glance. We must return and reexperience His death. Yes, and in doing so, die with Christ. Paul expressed it clearly: "For I am crucified with Christ . . ." (see Gal. 2:20). When we have so applied ourselves to His death, then we are prepared to focus ourselves on the living experience. Paul did not stop with dying: "For I am crucified with Christ, nevertheless I live . . ."

Without one question about the historicity of our Lord, we can still merely think of Him as a person who lived in the distant past. He lives today! (Yet, going back to the cross is necessary.) To stay there, as if the cross has no application to life today, is to fall short. We must go there long enough for our Lord to walk with us from the cross into our present day. To do this we can start with four sentences found in Luke 24:1-5 and Matthew 28:6-10. Let us lift them out and put them in an outline:

1. *They came unto the sepulchre, bringing the spices which they had prepared.*
2. *Why seek ye the living among the dead?*
3. *He is not here.*
4. *Ye shall see Him.*

Each one of these statements will serve as a major thought as we examine ourselves in light of what the cross means to us.

1. They came unto the sepulchre, bringing the spices which they had prepared.

It was the first day of the week. Christ was dead. The disciples had been scattered by the trauma of His death. Only a few women, and possibly John, had stayed by the side of their Lord. After His burial some of them began to gather. On that first Easter morning a handful of them went to the tomb where the body of Christ had been placed. There was no other place where they could nurse their hurt, or pay homage to Him Who had given them such hope. They were stunned by His apparent defeat and death, so they wended their way to the tomb, carrying their spices to perform the only duty of respect they could now offer.

For Christianity, death always precedes life. Although we will not stay among tombs, we might as well face them.

This third day after the resurrection, the disciples were possessed of an old attitude of God's people. "Our bones are dried, and our hope is lost" (Ezek. 37:11).

Christ's assailants had successfully executed their plans to rid themselves of the threat He posed, so they thought. They may have declared: "He is Dead! Dead! Dead!" No longer were they to be irritated by His non-conformity. His scathing denunciation of their elaborate religious orders was hushed. Thus, those who vehemently opposed Him felt freer to straddle their fences, there to crow of their victory. When the death blow was wielded, fear, uncertainty, and faithlessness cast their ominous shadows upon sincere hearts. Skepticism had a field day and haughtily boasted of its deadening effect.

The pity of it: Christ was dead to all! And no less dead to His own than to His enemies!

In struggling to overcome the nightmare of His death, a few disciples clung to reality. They must have wished to make the most of the dreadful defeat. All they knew to do was to return to "death valley." Upon their arrival, they were perplexed to discover an empty tomb where the body of their Lord had rested.

In our time, are we also facing a similar tomb? Inner fires cease to glow. The outward exercise of religious functions accelerates with air-beating gestures, but the power-glow of inner compulsion is gone. No spirit! No freshness! No urgency! Have our flesh died, our bones dried, and our hopes dimmed?

The similarity of these first disciples' experience equals many saddening epochs in the history of Christianity. Young heralds defect; old preachers grumble. The secular beat sets a strange pace for the newly merging society of Christians. A church's corruption does not smell when bathed in the intoxicating mixture of "success" and worldliness.

Here we stand among *these* whited sepulchres which indeed appear beautiful outwardly, but are within full of dead men's bones. Jesus has warned us about the dangers of giving attention only to appearing beautiful outwardly, and neglecting the inner spiritual qualities of life. He called the Pharisees to task and used the word *hypocrites* to describe such religious persons (see Matt. 23:27).

The gray shadows of uncertainty, doubt, and spiritual flippancy surround us. But worse than this are the blatant denials of the presence and power of God to change lives by the very ones who should be the vanguards of the faith. The agnosticism from pulpits and seats of theological learning chills the vital fires within sincere Christians. We are left with the tombs of prophets and garnished graves of the righteous.

Look at our spiritual decay. First, a biblical faith has been mocked. Some of us adopt slogans and mumble shibboleths as new revelation under the guise of freshness, relevancy, and progress. Call it what we will, we remain benumbed for the want of an authoritative certainty that somewhere, some way lets us know God is speaking!

Our spiritual decay is seen, secondly, in a formalistic religious activism. True, we did not want this, but routine patterns are established and made sacred. This even includes the informal church which has no written orders of service, prayer books, or liturgy guides. Yet they, too, follow a preciseness of ceremony equal to any congregation.

The presence of Christ is crushed by a false security caused by inward complacency and habits of outward observances which long since have lost their meaning, and it saddens us, because we never wanted this to happen. The form becomes the only resemblance to the sacred—that is, familiar musical tones and the same old words which are uttered with an exacting regularity of standing and sitting. The whole affair, once meaningful, useful, vibrant, and vital is now marred, defaced, and stripped of all its original worth. Religion—rather genuine Christianity—emptied of its spiritual meaning, and we never meant for it to be.

The need to "succeed" has pastors and other church leaders reeling under growing expectations. Success itself is not harming us, but the pressures from a perverted and unreal success syndrome are. The impact of unstated success standards is a reality. We can deny or ignore pressures to succeed. That does not lessen their influence. The reality bludgeons us by watching a pastor search committee set its standard for the kind of pastor it wants. The unstated success standards become painfully real. Let me put this matter of success out in the open and deal with it from a posture of our own choosing. Accepting and living with unreal and frustrating expectations are not necessary. Success cannot be equated with material growth, organizational size, and/or having a powerful position.

Phil Lineberger gives a good profile of a leader who keeps score by following the "marketplace" approach. This is described as a person who is expected to increase the gross national product of numbers of converts, church members, dollars, and victories from week to week.

Bob Burk, a pastor in Arkansas, believes our success values are borrowed from the world's standards of success. He thinks this results in the three "S's" of membership *size,* amount of *salary,* and number of *staff.*

Such opinions seem to be universal among church staff members. The translation of material wealth in a business corporation is seen in the general well-being of churches. This becomes the first order of business, the primary point of interest, and material wealth is the cue which symbolizes "the Lord is blessing us." Size, structure, and systems speak powerfully to the world's measure of success. When left alone and out of context, size, structure, and systems become ends in themselves. Empire-building, rather than building the kingdom, results. But the tragedy is: after we have built a worldly empire, we float out a few biblical words, wrap them around our glorious man-made empire, and call it God's kingdom. We finally end up in a lifeless, burned-out, and fruitless ministry, a graveyard of failure, not the life-giving "success" which we had hoped.

When applied to church leadership these kinds of power structures breed behavior which is strange to biblical Christianity. Securing a desired outcome overshadows the road we follow to reach there when worldly power structures are used. Expediency is justified by translating ill-advised methods into a spiritual language. This language serves to hide the lack of honesty and integrity.

But the last words have not been spoken. God is not muzzled. Amidst our quandary he sends messengers who cannot be shunned by any misplaced followers.

After the disciples went to the tomb, they found the stone rolled away from the sepulchre. They entered the tomb to see that the body of Jesus was gone. Then ". . . as they were much perplexed thereabout, behold, two men stood by them in shining garments" (Luke 24:4). These messengers came to point the way.

2. Why seek ye the living among the dead?

As we approach the sepulchre once sealed and secured by those who killed our Lord and who wish to expel *His kingdom* from the world, we may hear the thought-provoking, spirit-awakening question, "Why seek ye the living among the dead?" This could set in motion the supernatural rumbling from heaven as of a rushing mighty wind. Such a strange sound carries the spiritual vibrations of eternity—a voice heard above these dead men's bones! A voice carried on wings of fire creating a conviction of sin, pouring out the joys of forgiveness, and filling the mouths of God's people with a jubilant song.

Do you hear the question, "Why seek ye the living among the dead?"

What visionary defects would blind us so we cannot behold the obvious? Of course, we cannot hope to find the living among the dead—we never expected to! The dead can be resurrected—but they can never be revived. Destitution begats decay! And we have always known that. The Scriptures are so emphatic at this point.

If we expect malady to cure its own diseases, or darkness to dispel its own gloom, or death to defeat its own deadliness, then we are illogical.

If we think compromises with the Bible's truth will sound any sure note, or that spiritual weakness will take any firm stand, or that religious revolutionists will turn the world upside down for Christ, then we can never expect any ray of hope to shine through this dread gloom.

No, the living Christ is not to be found wrapped in the death clothes within an inanimate, cold, lifeless grave! The biblical record is clear. Christ will not be found in such a place.

We must turn elsewhere. Easy religion, elaborate liturgies, familiar routines, yesterday's revivals are poor substitutes. Let us not play the fool. We will seek Christ Himself. He is the Christ in history, the Christ of the Bible, the Christ of earth and heaven, the Christ who shall return, the Christ who lives now—here, in our hearts!

Down with the power structures formed by group-cliques in the name of a religion. Put away the so-called Christian "fellowship" which is shot through with ulterior motives. Kill that pride which gazes at the mammoth church structure as if it is the God its occupants know! Stop bannering success flags which scream "greater," "more," and "better." Down with the glory of gloating.

No, these posturings will never yield "the living"— and we had best stop looking here. We must hear the question, "Why seek ye the living among the dead?"

Where is that one red-hot coal in the dead ash heap, that it may be fanned afresh into a living fire? There is none here! And we must face it! The living cannot be found among the dead. We had not wanted this death, but now we behold the truth of it, and somehow our meager handful of spices becomes significantly worthless. No, we sincerely have meant to do the best we could. To hear this question, painful as it is, awakens us to a stark reality. We are looking in the wrong place!

3. He is not here!

At the bottom of despair's pit comes a fervent search for our souls. When we fall into this dreary shape, many are discouraged and even hostile. Others have consciences seared with the hot iron of skepticism, while a few choose to pamper the enemies of God to protect the vested interests of their dually-aligned lives. All of this is merely a futile effort to serve God.

On the other hand, our hopes may raise high as we launch on a venture to find a pot of gold at the end of a gorgeous rainbow. Suddenly we touch the truth: There is no gold—only a false promise at the end of a washed-out rainbow!

How much more was the anguish of the already heartsick disciples whose Lord had been crucified? They went to see for themselves. "He is not here!"

It would seem easier for them to believe He was not there, among the dead, than for us to believe He is not here among us. As we compare the Scriptures with our experiences, can we not face the dreadful truth? He is not here!

He is not here! But some may protest, "He has to be here; here—neatly laid away in our sweet-sounding religious phases. Our accurate vocabulary has always been the spiritual indicator which portrayed our Lord's blessings."

Not here? Impossible!

Others may shout, "He must be here! Else why such an abundance of energy displayed by incessant church activities? Look, the pulpit is not asleep. The ministry is at its peak in learning, culture, and ability. He must be here! Congregations are larger. Buildings are invitingly magnificent and programs are attractively elaborate."

In spite of all this, we hear the angelic voice announce: "He is not here! He is not here!"

However, to know He is not here may be a heavenly revelation. What a pity to find a person who will not admit he has the itch because he finds tremendous pleasure in scratching! So it is with Christians who have itching ears, or the poor persons who have so gradually and sometimes unwarily, put these good "second-rate trinkets" as priorities in their lives—and be so happy with that which is inferior. As good as some elements of our success standards, like buildings, budgets, and baptisms, they must be put in the right perspective, the rightful place. Our first love must surface and guide all other aspects of ministry. So much of our frantic activity cannot satisfy us or make worthly substitutes for an awareness of a living Lord. If it can, whether or not we want it, we are seeking life where there is no life, only tombs of the dead.

When we awaken to the reality which answers the question of why we seek the living among the dead, we are ready to hear another surety from the angelic visitors.

4. Ye shall see Him

We wait for an angel's voice to give us courage, hope and light. And it comes: "Ye shall see him."

Now we must pause to ask if we really want to receive this announcement. Seeing Him means facing the imperative of self-surrender, inner renewal, and personal commitment. Do we wish to pay the price of experiencing a broken heart and a contrite spirit? "The sacrifices of God are a broken spirit: a broken and a contrite heart, O God, thou wilt not despise" (Ps. 51:17). Can we dare hope for mere gifts without an absolute willingness to face the Giver? Must we back up to God with hands poised behind us, palms open to receive? We must face him—ready, waiting, willing. Like a wildfire, we must be willing to spread the good news once we see him. No conditions! No reservations!

Such awakenings must emerge from a siege through agony. This pain is the intense spiritual light which purges sin within the dark, dark crevices of our souls. The light reveals the blackness which hides the terrified and naked soul. Every dormant fault unconfessed; every deviation from truth for expediency's sake; every hopeless self-assertion laden with rationalized hypocrisy— all merging into a flood of terror. The horror of being caught in the very act!

> When I was ten years old a friend and I decided that the large, impressive, two-story house located back in an obscure wooded area needed its windows broken out. So we proceeded to throw stones through every window. With glass shattered and the job done, we ran away thinking the matter was ended.
>
> Not too many days later word was circulating in our little town that the owner of the house had offered a ten-dollar reward for information about the persons who broke the windows. I was not aware who owned the house

when we did the dirty work. He was a judge who lived nearby, a good friend of mine. He provided me with the equipment and his court to play tennis at my pleasure. Now, I had done him a severe wrong and felt deeply convicted of my crime.

I stopped playing tennis and avoided Mr. Marshall. The guilt grew beyond my ability to handle it. Fear and shame told me to hide what I had done. That only made matters worse. Then one day, Mr. Marshall walked out of the grocery store, and I unavoidably met him face to face. He greeted me exactly as I thought he would. "Morton, do you know who broke the windows in my house back in the woods?" I remember the experience releasing my guilt. "Mr. Marshall," I haltingly answered, "I have been wanting to tell you about that for days. I did it! I am sorry!" What an experience. Caught! Confessed! Cleansed! He forgave me.

My father provided a plan of restoration. Doing chores for Mr. Marshall every afternoon after school was pleasure. I was happy after my lingering, growing pain had been relieved by confession and cleansing. The same is true with the children of God, who like a little boy may find themselves hiding under the church steeple with the guilt of having shattered the commitment they once made to a living Lord.

Do we want to see Him? If so, the seizure of spiritual convulsions will prove therapeutic to our souls.

The terrible catalog of suppressed sin will be unlocked, and the pages will flash these hidden sins to a forgiving Lord.

This excruciatingly painful experience sweeps all the spiritual trash into one big heap and lays it before us as it is—unadorned. What a price to pay. But the weight must pound its force against our souls if we are to see Him.

To view my worthlessness, to stop the struggle of trying to live the impossible Christian life, to be fair with my Lord in Whom I trusted long ago, to say—"I do not care, except for Christ and His abiding will, moment by moment. My Lord lives in me"—is to know He will speak, work, and live in the likes of me!

I am driven to my knees to reclaim the presence of a Person I once found so real and alive. A crucified self, I die to all. The living Christ breaks forth in a glory which only God gives.

Jesus Christ presents himself to my world through me—and I shall submit!

It is worth it to see Him. Freedom floods my being. Here is life-giving rejuvenation for a sour and sick soul.

Now I see Him, the Lord Who lives in me. This is more than faith. It is life in the faith of the Son of God! More than a promise; it is a present event! More than an historical narrative; it is a personal reality! More than *something* to believe—it is *Someone* to live through me. It is the experience of Him living here—now! All of yesterday's experiences are but sweet memories and hard lessons. All of tomorrow's expectations are precious promises still out of reach. Christ is alive and real now, here—in me!

Here I am, Lord, without one plea! Without talent—or treasure. All that I am is found in the Lord who lives in me.

Out of an overwhelming compulsion, which surely was the breath of God, I searched for some revelation which may speak to me and my day. Well wrote Charlotte Elliott:

> Just as I am, without one plea,
>   But that Thy blood was shed for me,
> And that Thou bidd'st me come to Thee,
>   O Lamb of God, I come! I come!
>
> Just as I am, Thou wilt receive,
>   Wilt welcome, pardon, cleanse, relieve,
> Because Thy promise I believe,
>   O Lamb of God, I come! I come![1]

The new creature within me which had been cankered with a religious dry-rot is discharging the harmful waste. As a fresh new life grips me, it is met with assurance, confidence, and hope. Then the truth of Philippians 3:12 is stamped afresh upon my mind: "Not as though I had already attained, either were already perfect: But I follow after, if that I may apprehend that for which also I apprehended of Christ Jesus."

The sincere desire to find joy is being fulfilled. I see him! Risen . . . real . . . restoring . . . reviving. "Therefore let all the house of Israel know assuredly, that God hath made that same Jesus, whom ye have crucified, both Lord and Christ" (Acts 2:36).

Epilogue

Jesus Christ has made a difference because He is different. A comparative study of those who have left significant contributions in history reveals that Jesus Christ was one of a kind: more than a prophet, not merely a religious leader or simply a man with world-changing ideas. He was different. His cross, burial, and resurrection validated His differences, and made all He was and is and taught, legitimate and worthy of our faith in Him. That difference has a lasting effect. Through history that difference is still the driving force which changes our world today and will move on into eternity itself.

As we analyze the record of His life on earth we discover how different He was then, and how that difference was simple, but revolutionary. Humanity can never move beyond His impact.

Let us consider this Christ, whom millions of many nations, races, and cultures now embrace, and make Him Lord. Let us find out how His difference can make us different and with a perspective that counts now and forever. If we can follow His example we, too, can make a difference in our world. His life sets our pace. Look at Him, and decide how we can become like Him:

Yes, Jesus was different, but he did not let his differences stand in the way of loving people who were not like him.

As God's Son, He was sinless. Yet He mixed with and had sinners as His friends. Some people criticized Him for eating with sinners. Their difference did not make Him avoid them.

Jesus was a Jew, and thus a member of a minority group which was under strict Roman rule. He associated with the Romans, and even showed unusual kindness to Samaritans with whom Jews had no dealings. He did not let being a Jew make any difference.

Jesus was a carpenter. Yet He liked the politicians, fishermen, and religious leaders. He wanted to associate with people from all walks of life.

Jesus was single. Yet, he honored marriage and paid high tribute to women. He had no problems with being single, nor did He reject His manliness.

Jesus was a young person and died a young adult. Yet, He had time for people of all ages. He knew no generation gap.

Jesus taught us considerably about how to be humans. He did not claim any one life-style as the best. He practiced none of labeling people as "fancy city slickers" or "dumb country hicks." Jesus knew no wops, chinks, honkies, or niggers. Yet, He joined no minority rights movements.

Jesus was one of a kind. There never has been one like Him—nor will there ever be. Yes, He was different. But it was His love for all people—His ability to relate to everyone in any group anywhere—that made Him different. He dressed like everyone else. He had no special means of transportation, and no unusual house in which to live. He ate the same foods as others and in the same places. Still He was vastly different.

Jesus depended completely on His identity with His Heavenly Father. He declared, "My Father and I are one." He found His uniqueness not in the kind of music He liked or the part of the country in which He lived or in the school He attended or in the amount of money He had or in His race, color of skin, or manliness—or even in the "good old days," but rather in being at one with God the Father. Jesus emphasized in John 14:10, "The words I speak unto you I speak not of myself: but the Father that dwelleth in me doeth the works."

Some people did not want Jesus to be different. They wanted Him to be like them and because He was not, they crucified Him. And even concerning them Jesus requested, "Father, forgive them for they know not what they do."

The Crucifixion
by Jerome O. Williams

"There they crucified him" (Luke 23:33).

How full these words! What volumes are in them! How strategic the event here recorded! What pathos here expressed!

Each word in this brief text has a message. We seek to point out some thoughts which each word suggests.

The Place of the Crucifixion Was Calvary

There they crucified him. Think of all of the most historic places on earth, where people were born or died, treaties were signed, nations were founded, buildings were erected, agreements were made—and you will come back to Calvary and exclaim, "This is the most historic place on earth." Think of all the sacred places on earth, where marriage vows are said, where children are born, where bodies are buried, where the Lord saved, and you will come back to Calvary and proclaim, "This is the most sacred place on earth." Calvary is the place where Christ was crucified and died. The place is sacred and historic because of the importance to the human race of what happened there two millennia ago.

The People of the Crucifixion Were Cruel

There they crucified him. Those who nailed Jesus to the cross on Calvary were Jews and Romans. The rulers of the Jews passed the death sentence. The Jewish people cried again and again, "Crucify him! Crucify him!" and followed Him to Calvary, there to mock Him. Pilate, the Roman governor, delivered Him unto the mob to be crucified (John 19:16). The Roman centurion gave the orders, and the soldiers drove the nails into His flesh to pinion His body to the cross and raised the cross upright. The people who crucified Christ were cruel, but those who sin against Him now are guilty of the same crime, for He was crucified for all sinners. Sinners crucified Christ.

The Pain of the Crucifixion Was Cutting

There they crucified him. Crucified Christ! They stripped His garments from His body, placed His body on the cross, and drove vicious nails into His hands and feet. The blistering Syrian sun ceased to shine at noonday by the will of the sympathizing Father. Nailed to the cross, the body of Christ bled and suffered agony, even the agony as if all men were dying at one time. It was more than physical agony. It was more than the pain of the body. It was more than mental anguish. It was torment of soul. It was the suffering of the Son of God. Other men were crucified, but no other man could suffer as did Christ. In a remarkably short time Christ died on the cross. He "gave up the ghost" and commended His soul to the Father.

The Person of the Crucifixion Was Christ

There they crucified him. He came from God to earth to reveal the character of God to man. He was the one Person who had lived on earth among men, without sin. He came to do the will of God, and He did it perfectly, for He did always the things that pleased the Father. He was the Son of God. They crucified Christ. Christ surrendered His will to the will of the Father and died on the cross of Calvary.

The Purpose of the Crucifixion

"There they crucified him." "Christ died for our sins according to the scriptures" (1 Cor. 15:3). "The blood of Jesus Christ his Son cleanseth us from all sin" (1 John 1:7). "Jesus Christ . . . is the propitiation for our sins: and not for ours only, but also for the sins of the whole world" (1 John 2:2). Christ made atonement, paid the vicarious price, for all sins of all people of all the earth. His death makes it possible for all persons to be saved by grace through faith in Him, if only they would receive Him. No other death could mean so much for the people of the earth.

This brief text mentions the most sacred place, the most cruel people, the most painful death of the most important Person for the supreme purpose.[1]

Scriptures Related to
The Shadow of the Cross

The people which sat in darkness saw great light; and to them which sat in the region and shadow of death light is sprung up.

Matthew 4:16

Blood
For this is my blood of the new testament, which is shed for many for the remission of sins.

Matthew 26:28

And being in an agony prayed more earnestly: and his sweat was as it were great drops of blood falling down to the ground.

Luke 22:44

Then Jesus said unto them, Verily, verily, I say unto you, Except ye eat the flesh of the Son of man, and drink his blood, ye have no life in you.

John 6:53

Whoso eateth my flesh, and drinketh my blood, hath eternal life; and I will raise him up at the last day.

John 6:54

For my flesh is meat indeed, and my blood is drink indeed.

John 6:55

He that eateth my flesh, and drinketh my blood, dwelleth in me, and I in him.

John 6:56

Take heed therefore unto yourselves, and to all the flock, over the which the Holy Ghost hath made you overseers, to feed the church of God, which he hath purchased with his own blood.

Acts 20:28

Whom God hath set forth to be a propitiation through faith in his blood, to declare his righteousness for the remission of sins that are past, through the forbearance of God.

Romans 3:25

Much more then, being now justified by his blood, we shall be saved from wrath through him.

Romans 5:9

The cup of blessing which we bless, is it not the communion of the blood of Christ? The bread which we break, is it not the communion of the body of Christ?

1 Corinthians 10:16

After the same manner also he took the cup, when he had supped, saying, This cup is the new testament in my blood: this do ye, as oft as ye drink it, in remembrance of me.

1 Corinthians 11:25

Wherefore whosoever shall eat this bread, and drink this cup of the Lord, unworthily, shall be guilty of the body and blood of the Lord.

1 Corinthians 11:27

In whom we have redemption through his blood, the forgiveness of sins, according to the riches of his grace.

Ephesians 1:7

But now in Christ Jesus ye who sometimes were far off are made nigh by the blood of Christ.

Ephesians 2:13

And, having made peace through the blood of his cross, by him to reconcile all things unto himself; by him, I say, whether they be things in earth, or things in heaven.

Colossians 1:20

Neither by the blood of goats and calves, but by his own blood he entered in once into the holy place, having obtained eternal redemption for us.

Hebrews 9:12

For if the blood of bulls and of goats, and the ashes of an heifer sprinkling the unclean, sanctifieth to the purifying of the flesh.

Hebrews 9:13

How much more shall the blood of Christ, who through the eternal Spirit offered himself without spot to God, purge your conscience from dead works to serve the living God?

Hebrews 9:14

Saying, This is the blood of the testament which God hath enjoined unto you.

Hebrews 9:20

And almost all things are by the law purged with blood; and without shedding of blood is no remission.

Hebrews 9:22

Having therefore, brethren, boldness to enter into the holiest by the blood of Jesus.

Hebrews 10:19

Wherefore Jesus also, that he might sanctify the people with his own blood, suffered without the gate.

Hebrews 13:12

Now the God of peace, that brought again from the dead our Lord Jesus, that great shepherd of the sheep, through the blood of the everlasting covenant.

Hebrews 13:20

Elect according to the foreknowledge of God the Father, through sanctification of the Spirit, unto obedience and sprinkling of the blood of Jesus Christ: Grace unto you, and peace be multiplied.

1 Peter 1:2

But with the precious blood of Christ, as of a lamb without blemish and without spot.

1 Peter 1:19

And from Jesus Christ, who is the faithful witness, and the first begotten of the dead, and the prince of the kings of the earth. Unto him that loved us and washed us from our sins in his own blood.

Revelation 1:5

And I said unto him, Sir, thou knowest. And he said to me, These are they which came out of great tribulation, and have washed their robes, and made them white in the blood of the Lamb.

Revelation 7:14

Cross

And saying, Thou that destroyest the temple, and buildest it in three days, save thyself. It thou be the Son of God, come down from the cross.

Matthew 27:40

He saved others; himself he cannot save. If he be the King of Israel, let him now come down from the cross, and we will believe him.

Matthew 27:42

The God of our fathers raised up Jesus, whom ye slew and hanged on a tree.

Acts 5:30

And when they had fulfilled all that was written of him, they took him down from the tree and laid him in a sepulchre.

Acts 13:29

For Christ sent me not to baptize, but to preach the gospel: not with wisdom of words, lest the cross of Christ should be made of none effect.

1 Corinthians 1:17

For the preaching of the cross is to them that perish foolishness; but unto us which are saved it is the power of God.

1 Corinthians 1:18

But God forbid that I should glory, save in the cross of our Lord Jesus Christ, by whom the world is crucified unto me, and I unto the world.

Galatians 6:14

And that he might reconcile both unto God in one body by the cross, having slain the enmity thereby.

Ephesians 2:16

And, having made peace through the blood of his cross, by him to reconcile all things unto himself; by him, I say, whether they be things in earth, or things in heaven.

Colossians 1:20

Blotting out the handwriting of ordinances that was against us, which was contrary to us, and took it out of the way, nailing it to his cross.

Colossians 2:14

Looking unto Jesus the author and finisher of our faith; who for the joy that was set before him endured the cross, despising the shame, and is set down at the right hand of the throne of God.

Hebrews 12:2

Who his own self bare our sins in his own body on the tree, that we, being dead to sins, should live unto righteousness: by whose stripes ye were healed.

1 Peter 2:24

Crucified

Pilate saith unto them, What shall I do then with Jesus which is called Christ? They all say unto him, Let him be crucified.

Matthew 27:22

And the governor said, Why, what evil hath he done? But they cried out the more, saying, Let him be crucified.

Matthew 27:23

And they crucified him, and parted his garments, casting lots: that it might be fulfilled which was spoken by the prophet, They parted my garments among them, and upon my vesture did they cast lots.

Matthew 27:35

Saying, The Son of man must be delivered into the hands of sinful men, and be crucified, and the third day rise again.

Luke 24:7

And how the chief priests and our rulers delivered him to be condemned to death, and have crucified him.

Luke 24:20

Be it known unto you all, and to all the people of Israel, that by the name of Jesus Christ of Nazareth whom ye crucified, whom God raised from the dead, even by him doth this man stand here before you whole.

Acts 4:10

Knowing this, that our old man is crucified with him, that the body of sin might be destroyed, that henceforth we should not serve sin.

Romans 6:6

But we preach Christ crucified, unto the Jews a stumblingblock, and unto the Greeks foolishness.

1 Corinthians 1:23

For I determined not to know anything among you save Jesus Christ, and him crucified.

1 Corinthians 2:2

Which none of the princes of this world knew: for had they known it, they would not have crucified the Lord of glory.

1 Corinthians 2:8

For though He was crucified through weakness, yet he liveth by the power of God. For we also are weak in him, but we shall live with him by the power of God toward you.

2 Corinthians 13:4

I am crucified with Christ: nevertheless I live; yet not I, but Christ liveth in me: and the life which I now live in the flesh I live by faith of the Son of God, who loved me, and gave himself for me.

Galatians 2:20

Crucify

If they shall fall away, to renew them again unto repentance; seeing they crucify to themselves the Son of God afresh, and put him to an open shame.

Hebrews 6:6

Death

And the chief priests and scribes sought how they might kill him; for they feared the people.

Luke 22:2

And he said unto them the third time, Why, what evil hath he done? I have found no cause of death in him: I will therefore chastise him, and let him go.

Luke 23:22

Him, being delivered by the determinate counsel and foreknowledge of God, ye have taken, and by wicked hands have crucified and slain.

Acts 2:23

And killed the Prince of life, whom God hath raised from the dead; whereof we are witnesses.

Acts: 3:15

And we are witnesses of all things which he did both in the land of the Jews, and in Jerusalem; whom they slew and hanged on a tree.

Acts: 10:39

And though they found no cause of death in him, yet desired they Pilate that he should be slain.

Acts 13:28

For if, when we were enemies, we were reconciled to God by the death of his Son, much more, being reconciled, we shall be saved by his life.

Romans 5:10

For if we have been planted together in the likeness of his death, we shall be also in the likeness of his resurrection.

Romans 6:5

Knowing that Christ being raised from the dead dieth no more; death hath no more dominion over him.

Romans 6:9

For in that he died, he died unto sin once: but in that he liveth, he liveth unto God.

Romans 6:10

That I may know him, and the power of his resurrection, and the fellowship of his sufferings, being made conformable unto his death.

Philippians 3:10

In the body of his flesh through death, to present you holy and unblameable and unreproveable in his sight.

Colossians 1:22

But is now made manifest by the appearing of our Saviour Jesus Christ, who hath abolished death, and hath brought life and immortality to light through the gospel.

2 Timothy 1:10

But we see Jesus who was made a little lower than the angels for the suffering of death, crowned with glory and honour; that he by the grace of God should taste death for every man.

Hebrews 2:9

Forasmuch then as the children are partakers of flesh and blood, he also himself likewise took part of the same; that through death he might destroy him that had the power of death, that is, the devil.

Hebrews 2:14

For where a testament is, there must also of necessity be the death of the testator.

Hebrews 9:16

Notes

Introduction

1. J. W. MacGorman, *Layman's Bible Book Commentary,* Vol. 20 (Nashville, TN: Broadman Press, 1982), p. 144.

2. Words by J. Wilbur Chapman

3. Joseph Klausner, *Jesus of Nazareth* (New York: The Macmillan Co., 1929), p. 349.

Chapter 1

1. D. P. Brooks, *Dealing with Death: A Christian Perspective* (Nashville, TN: Broadman Press, 1974), p. 20.

2. Rick Norman, *Poems of Encouragement* (Nashville: Broadman Press, 1982), p. 15.

3. Words by Stuart K. Hine © Copyright 1953, 1955, Renewed 1981 by Manna Music, Inc. Used by permission.

4. Fisher Humphreys, Editor, *Nineteenth Century Evangelical Theology, Christian Classics* (Nashville: Broadman Press, 1981), p. 248.

5. Ibid.

6. Leslie F. Brandt, *Epistles Now* (St. Louis, MO: Concordia Publishing House, 1976), p. 137.

Chapter 2

1. Karen Burton Mains, *Karen! Karen!* (Wheaton, IL: Tyndale House Publishers, Inc., 1974), p. 54.

2. Words by Lewis E. Jones.

Chapter 3

1. Lewis B. Smedes, *Forgive and Forget* (San Francisco, Harper & Row Publishers, 1984), p. xi.

Chapter 4

1. Words by Robert Lowry.

2. Words by Francis H. Rowley.

Chapter 5

1. From *Treasury of the Christian Faith,* Edited by Stanley I. Stuber and Thomas Clark (New York: Association Press, 1949), p. 211.

2. Humphreys, Ibid., p. 255*ff.*

3. Ibid.

4. Ibid.

Chapter 6

1. Words by Charlotte Elliott.

Epilogue

1. Jerome O. Williams, *Seeds for Sermons* (Nashville: Broadman Press, 1945), pp. 34-36.